Italy, already so rich in history and beauty has another treasure — its contemporary writers. Amongst them are Leonardo Sciascia and his Sicilian murder-mysteries, Pasolini with his tales of Roman low-life as well as brilliant women writers like Natalia Ginzburg and Dacia Maraini.

The Babel Guide is your key to this wide world of reading — inside are details on *all* Italian novels and short stories available in English with 129 'trailers' to the best books of over 70 writers to aid your purchasing or borrowing choices.

Take a journey to the heart of Italy; here is the guide.

'a brilliant idea'
— Paul Hyland, BBC Radio 3

The Babel Guide to
ITALIAN
Fiction
(in English Translation)

by Ray Keenoy & Fiorenza Conte
with
Helen Blücher-Altona
Michael Caesar
Patrick Curry
Lola Rinvolucri
Michèle Roberts

Illustrations by Jackie Wrout

BOULEVARD

Babel Guide to Italian Fiction in English Translation

©Boulevard Books 1995.
First published 1995 by Boulevard Books
8 Aldbourne Road
London W12 OLN, UK
Tel/Fax 0181 743 5278

Special thanks to

Helen Blücher-Altona
Michael Caesar
Patrick Curry
Flavia Gentili
Piero Leodi
Siân Williams
Jackie Wrout

ISBN 1 899460 00 4

Boulevard Books are distributed in the UK by Central Books.

Cover Art: Chris Hyde
Typeset & Design: Studio Europa
Printed and bound by the Guernsey Press, Guernsey, C.I.

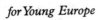

for Young Europe

CONTENTS

Introducing the Babel Guides...

This is the first of the Babel Guides, a new series of books which list and discuss fiction in translation available in English, country by country, with the accent on contemporary writing. This edition focuses on Italy and is in two parts — the *Database* section has the details of all the books by Italian authors translated since 1945 and the *Reviews* section introduces over a hundred of the best of them with a carefully selected quotation to give you a taste of the writing.

The Babel Guides are here to help readers, librarians and booksellers to locate and appreciate international literature by emphasizing the new foreign writing amidst the mass of titles available today. We're sure that having this information in an accessible, portable form will enrich and extend your reading.

The Quality of Light

Eds. A & M Caesar

This new anthology includes a whole batch of writers under forty, many of them previously unpublished in English: the Chekovian Tondelli with his story of Italian junkies and deadbeats who hang around in *The Station Bar*; Sandro Veronesi with his very short *A Worthwhile Death*, the witty Pia Fontana and the highly esteemed Daniel Del Guidice.

There's a good dose in this anthology of the political, critical fiction that the Italians seem to do so much better than us; as in the light touch of Enrico Palandri's *PEC* or the awareness of other people's history in Vincenzo Consolo's *The Photographer*. Italians do have more political consciousness than Anglo-Saxons, (even if this rarely produces any great results in practice) and left-wing dailies such as *L'Unità* and *Il Manifesto* regularly publish short stories by excellent young writers like Valeria Viganò, Sandro Veronesi and Sandra Petrignani.

The Quality of Light serves as tasty appetiser to a world of exciting, youthful writing pleasantly different from the local product provided by English and American publishers. This is an excellent, rich collection — our only grouse is that apart from Piera Oppezza's strange and clever scene of 'double-intimacy' and the doomed Tondelli's pimpish-punkish toilet sex, the stories gathered here would never lead the innocent reader to guess what a *sensual* nation the Italians are. RL

'The child has a mouth like a suction cup, its hair is sweaty from crying, she holds it with rigid arms and her unbuttoned shirt shows her body down to her navel, her face and hair are devastated by sleep. A witch, a feverish witch in the night and perhaps her milk is a subtle poison, as sticky as the juice of certain plants of the swamps. The lady stayed there and watched her, uncertainly fingering the tin of talcum powder, then the little pink hairbrush, the bottle of Sangemini water, her long silk nightdress which gleams among the lilies of Florence.' p7 *The Wet Nurse* Rosetta Loy

ANTHOLOGY

New Italian Women

Ed. Martha King

A combination of new and previously published translations of short stories and novel-extracts, this selection represents what King calls 'mature writers of the 1980s'. Among the heavyweights of Italian female art-fiction such as Anna Maria Ortese, Grazia Deledda and Elsa Morante and the stalwarts of more populist writing such as Dacia Maraini and Giuliana Morandini sparkle some lesser-known names such as Geda Jacolutti and Marina Mizzau. This anthology is a very valuable sampler of what was being written up to the time of publication in 1989, issued by the Italica Press, an excellent small publisher specialising in *Italica*. RL

'At that time refined and vampish men were the fashion and our French teacher interpreted the type with a lavish style and a little *disengagé*. In class the girls watched him in fascination, madness. I observed the desk and the actor who rested his moist, pseudo-distracted look upon us from the platform and, annoyed at seeing how the others admired him, I found it easier to play the insolent student. He spoke slowly, in a nasal voice, putting out his half-smoked cigarette before beginning to read a poet, and from time to time interrupting his reading to make some ironic or sentimental comment. The girls gazed at his eyes and hair and whispered "a mouth to bite" among themselves, according to the manner of that age. I chose the moment of highest enchantment to act: I let a dictionary crash to the floor with a calculated clatter and responded with dry provocation to the rebuke from the desk.' p59 *The French Teacher* Geda Jacolutti

ANTHOLOGY

Short Stories From Abruzzo

Eds. George Talbot & Dante Marinacci

An unusual book: a labour of love by a group of Dublin-based admirers of Italian culture. The stories all come from the Abruzzo, a rural and formerly very isolated region lost up in the mountains East of Rome. Given its tiny catchment area, the collection is quite variable, with some stunning pieces such as Anna Maria D'Alessandro's *Far Away To Learn* and

Maria Teresa Falconi's *Waiting*, an account of single women's lives, as well as stories that read as documents of social change, like the biographical *The Embrace* with its picture of the recent history of the coastal region. All in all a unique and worthwhile work. RL

'I have been a nervous barefoot little girl, brought up on hills full of peaches and cherries, in a country shop, among barrels of herring and boxes of cigars. In the afternoons during July, the earth breathed again, the leaves of the olive trees used to lose their astonishing immobility, silvering the hills, and the Maiella, like a bride, reflected the light of the sunset, timorously longing for the embrace of the sun.' p113   *Far Away To Learn* D'Alessandro

ANTHOLOGY

Italian Short Stories [Racconti Italiani 1]

Ed. Raleigh Trevelyan

This selection was originally published in 1965, a date which gives it a good overview of the intensely creative period of Italian literature (and cinema) that ran from the late fascist era up to the early 1960s — such an important epoch that only now is another generation of younger writers emerging (who are represented in the Serpent's Tail anthology reviewed above). The writers included here; Italo Calvino, Carlo Cassola, Carlo Emilio Gadda, Natalia Ginzburg, Alberto Moravia, Cesare Pavese, Vasco Pratolini and Mario Soldati — are all (apart from Soldati, a very good minor writer) still considered as important; Calvino, for one, has influenced writers around the world with his stylistic innovations.

The book is published in 'parallel text', with each story appearing in English opposite the Italian original. It's a pleasant way for the student of Italian to develop the ability to read Italian prose and increase vocabulary, but the quality of the stories is so high that it's worth finding a copy just to read in English. The most effective story is perhaps Natalia Ginzburg's The Mother, an alternative vision of motherhood and family life written circa 1957. RL

'She told them they must turn the other way while she undressed, they heard the quick rustle of her clothes, and shadows danced on the walls; she slipped into bed beside them, her thin body in its cold silk nightdress, and they moved away from her because she always complained that they came too close and kicked while they slept; sometimes she put out the light so that they should go to sleep and smoked in silence in the darkness.' pp109-110 *The Mother* Natalia Ginzburg

ANTHOLOGY

Italian Short Stories [Racconti Italiani 2]

Ed. Dmitri Vittorini

Although published in 1970 the second parallel text book of Italian stories is 50% composed of wartime stories which, while including Mario Rigoni-Stern's moving *Nikolayevka,* a tale of the Italian forces that fought in Russia 1941-1943 alongside Hitler's battalions, are perhaps less interesting to English-speaking readers saturated with books, films and TV programmes of vainglorious war nostalgia.

However there are also present in this collection marvellous pieces such as *The Tart* by Pasolini, a harsh tale of a Dickensian world but without Dickens' good guys, an outrageous story by Italo Svevo *The Mother* and part of Elio Vittorini's *Wartime Autobiography* on becoming a writer. RL

'I had not forgotten *Robinson Crusoe,* which I had read at the age of seven in an abridged edition for children. Every time I had managed to get hold of a fuller translation, I had without fail read it again. And I would have liked to read it in the original. I would have liked to read everything Defoe wrote. In the printing works of *La Nazione* there was half an hour's spare time between the moment when the real work stopped and the moment when we could clock out and go home. Some workers spent this half hour doing crossword puzzles, others talking about football, others reading and even studying. My friend who knew English agreed to teach me the language. And we began in rather an unusual way. We worked on the text of *Robinson Crusoe,* reading it and translating word by word, writing over each English word its Italian equivalent.... Afterwards I went on alone, rather like a deaf-mute, using other texts by Defoe and by eighteenth- and nineteenth- century writers, contemporary writers and American ones, too, until at last I felt capable of translating correctly.' p45 *Wartime Autobiography; On Becoming A Writer* Elio Vittorini

D'ANNUNZIO
Gabriele

The Triumph Of Death [Il Trionfo Della Morte]

Taking its title from a series of Pisan frescoes attributed to
Buffalmacco, this is the first Italian novel to celebrate
Nietzsche's theory of the superman — represented here by
D'Annunzio's hero Giorgio Aurispa. Gripped by a deathwish,
Aurispa finds his intellectual vocation to be a writer impeded
by an earthly and physical desire, his excessive and entirely
carnal love for Ippolita Sanzio. A fascination with death
shrouds the entire story, whose thread is provided by the
protagonist's infirmity of will. This weakness prevents him
from shaking off his creative block and freeing himself from
the damnation of an insane passion for a woman who is
sensually unbalanced.

Aurispa's attempts to escape from Ippolita by returning to
the past in his home town and the undefiled Abruzzi countryside are useless, as are his attempts to set up a new life with
Ippolita as devotees of a superstitious and primitive
Christianity preached by peasant cultists. Contact with nature and the genuine soul of the people fails to cure either
Aurispa's intellectual impotence or his sexual subjugation,
but it exposes him to the sordid reality of a life of degradation
which he finds unacceptable. Suicide remains the only type
of heroism available to him, and he draws his lover in too —
tragic gesture of the intellectual in the face of failure, the bitter conclusion being that the words and vision which would
make creativity possible for him are snatched away by the rise
of a vulgar, arrogant society, the domination of money and
the carnal torment which has reduced him to sterility.

As the vision of a writer who wanted to produce 'total art',
this fragment of Aurispa's life is an exceptional document of
an intellectual consciousness which, at the end of the nineteenth century, had to face the loss of its role in society. This
was a society whose only ideal was economic and political
aggrandisement — similar perhaps to our own *fin de siècle* of
the 1980s and 90s. FC

'When in the dawn of the great day, Giorgio Aurispa awoke out of an
uneasy slumber, his first thought was: 'She is coming to-day! In this day's
light I shall behold her, clasp her in my arms! It seems as if to-day she will

be mine for the first time — I feel as if I could die of it!' The vision he called up sent a sudden thrill through him from head to foot, like an electric shock, and the terrible physical phenomenon came upon him, against whose tyranny he knew himself to be utterly powerless. His whole being succumbed to the despotism of his senses, once again his inherited sensuality blazed up with irresistible fury in this fastidious and delicate-minded lover, who delighted to call his mistress sister, and yearned for spiritual communion with her. One by one he mentally reviewed her several beauties, and each outline, seen through the flame of his desire, assumed a radiance, a splendour that was chimerical, almost superhuman. He contemplated in spirit her every caress; every attitude was replete with fascination — in her all was light and perfume and rhythm.

And this adorable creature was his — his alone! But with that, on a sudden, like the smoke from a dull fire, the demon of jealousy rose in his mind. To shake it off he jumped out of bed. pp131-132

The Flame *aka* The Flame Of Life [Il Fuoco]

The love story between Nietzschean 'superman' poet and musician Stelio Effrena and ageing actress La Foscarina (the literary counterpart of the great Eleonora Duse) unfurls beneath the symbol of fire, creator and destroyer of life. The backdrop to the couple's passionate affair is the city of Venice, which, described in autumnal colours of mists and sunsets as an enchanting city of decadence, ruin and death, almost becomes a character itself in this story. In the slow and implacable disintegration of the city La Foscarina sees her own old age sneaking up on her, while Stelio Effrena anticipates the idea of the death of art — supplanted by utilitarian logic in the new world of the *bourgeois*.

The Flame can be read as a tale of passion or as an aesthetic debate on the future of art, but it is above all a portrait of Stelio Effrena: the Commander, the image-maker, he who knows no bounds, ruling everything and rejecting everything, indifferent to the pain he causes, living up to his motto 'create with joy'. His driving force is a fire which burns as it creates, transforming the world's degeneracy into art. Whereas Thomas Mann's Aschenbach collapses amid the death and decay of Venice, Effrena accepts the same conditions as a challenge: salvation comes through fire that, as in Venice's Murano glass-works, purifies material and regenerates it, rescuing it from the clutches of corruption. FC

'Stelio quivered as though she had unexpectedly touched him. Once again the expressive power of her prophetic lips aroused an ideal image from some indefinable depths that rose up as though from a tomb before the poet's gaze, and took on the colour and breath of life... It was an apparition of fire, bolder and more dazzling than that which had lit up the harbour of San Marco, a flaming life-force, flung from the deepest womb of nature towards the expectant throng, a vehement zone of light erupting from an inner sky to illuminate the most secret depths of human desire and the human will, a word that has never been spoken, come from primeval silence to express all that is eternal and eternally unsayable in the heart of the world.' p90

The Victim [L'Innocente]

This is a confessional novel whose protagonist, Tullio Hermil, recounts the crime he has committed. Believing himself to be an exceptional man, a rare spirit, he allows himself, by virtue of this presumed uniqueness, to indulge in a series of marital infidelities. But on discovering that his wife Giuliana is expecting a child (the consequence of a moment of weakness on her part) he is forced to confront a breakdown in the normal order of his life and marriage. His resulting frame of mind, a combination of wounded pride and phony repentance, leads him to devise a 'great plan' to eliminate the fruit of sin and feminine transgression, eventually driving him to cause the death of the newborn baby. His futile hope is to regain his commanding position (which Giuliana's deed has compromised, in spite of her overwhelming remorse) through the restoration of a self-love which overcomes all sense of guilt and aspires to a reciprocal purification. In fact, the crime only sets the final seal on a more drastic and hopeless guilt in both parties, consigning both to a deep grief without hope of atonement.

This book, made into an exquisite film by Lucchino Visconti, shifts the themes of the great Russian novels to an Italian environment, with alternating backdrops of *fin-de-siècle* cityscapes and untainted rural life as symbol of purity. D'Annunzio's meditation on the guilt ravaging Hermil's selfish soul could have been inspired by Dostoevsky, while from Tolstoy came the Christian vision of life, out of reach of these protagonists but shared by the minor characters and countryfolk, witnesses to the goings-on in the country mansion. FC

'We both turned towards the garden and listened. The garden had melted into a confused dim mass of violet, broken only by the dull gleam of the pond. There still remained a band of light on the extreme edge of the sky: a broad tricoloured zone, blood-red below, then orange, then dead-leaf green. Through the silence of the twilight, a voice rang clear and liquid like the first notes of a flute.

It was the nightingale... We listened with our eyes fixed upon the distant band of colour fading slowly behind the impalpable veil of evening. My soul hung suspended on that sound as if I looked for some great revelation of love from it. And the poor creature at my side — what were her feelings during those moments of listening? To what depths of anguish did she descend?' p125

Child of Pleasure [Il Piacere]

At the heart of this novel set among a turn-of-the-century Roman aristocracy engulfed in its own decadence stands Andrea Sperelli, a refined and worldly poet. Sperelli is entangled by two conflicting loves: firstly, for the sensual Elena Muti and, secondly, for the spiritual Maria Ferres, who represents the experience of art and poetry. In the end cynicism and sensual passion triumph as Sperelli calls out Elena's name during a night of love with Maria, who flees in horror. The spiritual-artistic vocation is thereby vanquished by the erotic and moral principle is replaced by a cult of sterile aestheticism which reflects the ethical perspective of the nineteenth-century decadents.

Inspired by Joris-Karl Huysman's *A Rebours* (Against Nature), the book concludes with a sense of failure as Sperelli the 'superior man' has to confront his own unstable nature, wayward and chameleon-like and incapable of fulfilling itself spiritually in real life. FC

'During this pause, both felt a certain perplexing uneasiness; Elena was no longer exactly conscious of the moment, nor was she quite mistress of herself... In the presence of this man to whom, once upon a time, she had been bound by such passionate ties, and in this spot where she lived the most ardent moments of her life, she felt her reserve melting, her mind wavering and growing feeble. She was at that dangerously delicious point of sentiment at which the soul receives its every impulse, its attitudes, its form from its external surroundings as an aerial vapour from the mutations of the atmosphere.' p197

ANTONIONI
Michelangelo

That Bowling Alley On The Tiber [Quel Bowling Sul Tevere]

This book is a collection of short essays and sketches of ideas for films. The latter will undoubtedly never be made but in their own way they provide as valuable an insight into Antonioni's mental world as the films he did complete.

That world is strangely postmodern, although he was working well before the term became popular. As a child in Ferrara, he writes, 'in winter, when the fog moved in, I liked walking the streets. It was the only moment when I could think I was somewhere else.' Antonioni's adult world, too, is one, as he puts it, 'where nothing is conclusive.' As his translator points out, 'Reality, like truth, is attainable, but only temporarily, provisionally so.'

The protagonists in Antonioni's films, from *Blow Up* and *The Passenger* to *The Identification Of A Woman*, are all caught up in the process of self-realisation, forever incomplete because they are (in principle) endless — fog, in fact, is a recurrent image in his work. Their stories, too, are only loosely narrative: beginnings, middles and ends are transparent conventions, pervaded by a sense of their own contingency.

The same is true of Antonioni himself. One of his principle working methods, he explains, is to 'start looking at things,' then work 'backwards from a series of images to a state of affairs.' And there is, of course, always more than one possible state of affairs that would explain any series of images. So one could say that in a further erosion of rigid conventions worthy of Ionesco or Flann O'Brien, Antonioni lives in the same world as his protagonists. As do we, when we participate in his films — this book is another way in to, or perhaps out of them. PC

'At the end of September night on the plain comes swiftly. Day ends when the headlights unexpectedly flick on. A little earlier the sunset had spread a magical light over the brick walls and it was the city's metaphysical moment. That was the hour when the women came out. In the cities of the Po Valley women were a category of reality. The men waited for twilight in order to see them. The men were greatly attached to money, they were crafty and lazy, with the rhythm of tedium. If money made them restless, women soothed them. In the Po Valley men loved women with irony. At twilight they watched them walking by, and the women knew it. At night you saw groups of men standing on the sidewalks to talk. They were talking about women. Or money.

The film I had in mind dealt with a strange story between a man and a woman in Ferrara. Strange to those who aren't natives of this city. Only a citizen of Ferrara can understand a relationship that lasted eleven years without even existing.' p43

BALESTRINI
Nanni

The Unseen [Gli Invisibili]

The early 1970s were years when Italian cities reverberated with political chants, wildcat strikes and utopian demands. Everlasting meetings convened in dry, dusty rooms full of cigarette smoke, with many of the young participants busy looking for ways to get by without regular jobs, spinning out their college careers. This was the time the Italians call the 'Years of Conflict' (*gli anni di contestazione*) or, more bleakly, the 'Years of Lead' (as in bullets).

Balestrini's *The Unseen* is a personal, grimly accurate testament to that period. The story it tells — recalled from inside the riotous mayhem of a maximum security prison full of young 'politicals' — is of a working-class youngster living and participating in that half-demented, half-amazing era. The protagonist starts as an idealist working for social justice but is eventually dragged into a circle of gun-toting fanatics who have left any original ideals far behind in their talk of power and violence.

As well as its atmosphere of slogans and tear gas, *The Unseen* offers convincing documentation of the unglamorous side of the boom years that preceded the wild 1970s. What Balestrini doesn't transmit so well is the youthful optimism (and, perhaps, the ridiculous arrogance) that made this generation believe it was on the threshold of a new world it would some-how manage to build out of songs and dreams. He does however accurately describe how rapidly (and strangely) a large-scale movement in Italy was precipitated into isolated acts of violent terrorism, a wave of bombings and assassinations by 'revolutionary armed bands', most notoriously the 'Brigate Rosse' (Red Brigades) and how revolutionary dreams ended for some in long years of incarceration ordered by a political establishment that was alternately cruel and frightened, bewildered and devious. A mess and a morass, and one it would be good to be able to say that Italy is well out of — but with almost the entire political and economic élite of the nation exposed as being up to their necks in corruption when will it be possible to say that? RL

'the streets are busy all the time with groups of comrades the evenings are high-spirited lively noisy with our sounds shouts songs music they're made colourful by our jackets scarves skirts hats the walls are one long stretch of graffiti...with slogans one on top of the other against the bosses against sweated labour against all work against the ghettos against the clergy against the mayor against the trade unions against the parties against the city council against men against heroin against fascists against cops against judges against the state...against the family against school against sacrifices against boredom.' p173

BANTI
Anna

Artemisia [Artemisia]

The Artemisia of the title is the painter Artemisia Gentileschi, who was active in the first half of the seventeenth century but recognised as a great artist only seventy years ago by the critic Roberto Longhi. An ardent disciple of Caravaggio, Gentileschi worked in Florence and Rome, taught painting in Naples, travelled in England and, when, hardly more than a child, was subjected to public trial after being the victim of a rape. Neither historical novel nor literary biography, Banti's book offers a compensation of sorts to a person too long unfairly ignored.

The first draft was lost beneath the bombs, whereupon Banti wrote a second draft in the form of an 'open diary'. The story of the forgotten painter alternates with the writer's apprehension at rewriting a work and determination for a reciprocal rescue. Banti finds a correspondent in Gentileschi, a sister in art, someone with whom to share dreams, resentments and passions in the belief that women artists have always risked being doomed to obscurity. The result is a confession, part-truth and part-invention, both biography and autobiography; one of the strangest and most demanding novels in the whole spectrum of Italian literature. FC

'Under the rubble of my house I have lost Artemisia, my companion from three centuries ago who lay breathing gently on the hundred pages I had written. At the same time as I recognize her voice, hordes of swirling images pour out...images, at first, of a disillusioned and despairing Artemisia before she died...images, all of them crystal clear and sharp, sparkling under a May sun. Artemisia as a child, skipping among the artichokes in the monks' garden on Pincio hill, a stone's throw from her house; Artemisia as a young girl, shut in her room, holding her handkerchief over her mouth to stifle her sobs; and hot-tempered, her hand raised in anger, calling down curses with knitted brow; and a young beauty, with bent head and a faint smile on her lips, all dressed up in a slightly severe gown...' p4

BASSANI
Giorgio

Behind The Door [Dietro la Porta]

Set, like *Garden Of The Finzi-Continis*, in Bassani's native city of Ferrara, these are the experiences and feelings of a competitive, intelligent schoolboy growing up in the early 1930s. Bassani demonstrates his brilliance as a writer, his skill in evoking worlds, the thrill of little triumphs like being top of the class in maths, the confused fascination felt for a schoolfriend's beautiful mother...There isn't the elegiac melancholy of *Garden* here but prepare to be absorbed nevertheless by William Weaver's lively, charming translation. RL

'...they didn't give a damn, Legnani and Bertoni: the first was about to get married — so we heard — and the second, with her wasp waist, her black shiny bangs, and her malicious eyes like the movie star Elsa Merlini's, would hardly sit through the Fifth again. She was the sort to slip off to Rome and become an actress — as we had heard her declare many a time — instead of staying there to gather mould behind the door of the Liceo!' p8

Garden Of The Finzi-Continis [Il Giardino degli Finzi-Continis]

This story is set in the fascist era of the 20s and 30s. The garden lies behind a villa in the prosperous Northern city of Ferrara and is the centre of the happy world of Alberto and Micòl, children of a wealthy Jewish family. Walled away from the ominous rumbles of an Italy slipping more and more under the influence of Nazi Germany, their world eventually shrinks to just this garden — a metaphor for the extirpation of their own lives and that of their community. As their horizons draw in, Alberto slowly sickens and dies of a mysterious wasting disease while the spirited and beautiful Micòl gradually relinquishes both her brilliant career — all professions were closed to Italy's Jewish citizens after 1938 — and, sensing that she has no future, renounces any fruitful love.

Bassani's book is a tender, delicate requiem for a drowned world of beauty and intelligence, a diverse and cosmopolitan way of being Italian that Italy robbed itself of, leaving it a country that shares, if to a lesser degree, the curious postwar 'moral vacuum' of Germany; a nation on parole, frightened of its own misdeeds and yet also frightened to own up to them.

What makes this requiem effective is the way it transcends these particular events and celebrates the mysteries of beauty, intelligence, friendship and kindness, which are thrown into relief by a melancholy destiny. RL

'When I went back...at the beginning of May I found spring bursting out everywhere, the sprawling fields between Alessandria and Piacenza already yellow, the country lanes of Emilia full of girls out on bicycles, already bare-armed and bare-legged, the great trees along the walls of Ferrara already in leaf.' p183

The Gold-rimmed Spectacles [Gli Occhiali d'Oro]

This book is about two different but parallel experiences of isolation: that of a distinguished, homosexual professional, Doctor Fadigati, and that of the young Jewish student who feels an affinity with the doctor because of the imposition of the racial laws of 1938 (which banned Jewish Italians from practising professions). The backdrop, as in all Bassani's novels, is Ferrara, whose provincial, enclosed society finds a renewed strength in fascism and a new vigour in sanctioning repressive legislation. But though this collective acquiescence drives Doctor Fadigati to suicide, for the young man it constitutes the complex moment which forms his consciousness. He recognises that the persecution of Fadigati is another form of the persecution directed at him, and the solidarity he develops with the doctor forms the core of the novel.

Bassani's skill as a writer finds full expression in this book, in which the voice that denounces the ideology of fascism is amplified into a more profound reflection on man and his relationship with evil. The blame that people attribute to what is different, their lack of charity and tolerance together with an appetite for oppression, are the themes inscribed in the story of the doctor whose glinting gold-rimmed spectacles give the book its title. FC

'After a hard day's work he liked to feel himself in the crowd: the gay, noisy, neutral crowd. Tall and fat, with his soft hat, his yellow gloves and, in winter, his long loose cloak lined with opossum and his walking-stick hooked into the right pocket beside the sleeve, between eight and nine in the evening he might be seen anywhere in town. Sometimes you might be surprised to see him standing in front of a shop-window in Via Mazzini or Via Saraceno, peering intently over the shoulders of the man in front of him. Often he stood by the stands of knickknacks and sweets that spread in dozens along the south side of the cathedral, or in Piazza Travaglio, or in Via Garibaldi, staring silently at the unpretentious goods on show. But the narrow, crowded pavements of Via San Romano were those that Fadigati liked best. By those low doorways, smelling acridly of fried fish, salted foods, wine and cheap rope, and crowded with girls and soldiers, boys and cloaked peasants, it was strange to see his gay, lively, satisfied look, when you met him, and the vague smile that lit up his face.' p15 (I. Quigley tr.)

The Heron [L'Airone]

The protagonist of this psychological novel personifies the post-liberation (1945) generation and the frustration of the ideals experienced in those years; Bassani follows a day in the life of Edgardo Limentani — his last day. It's a long, drawn-out day in which memories of his past that have been soothed by time and emotions which he has long pursued but never captured come floating to the surface as he hunts in the Po delta near Ferrara, an unending landscape of plains and water. From the hide where he awaits his prey, Limentani, a lawyer, suddenly sees a heron flying unhurriedly across the sky. One cruel shot brings the creature plunging to the ground, with the intention of turning its solemn, graceful beauty into an object stuffed with straw. The wounded heron's attempts to stay alive are futile, and become in Edgardo's eyes a symbol of human suffering, of man's vain efforts to acquire values that he has been stripped of from the start and that only death can give back in the frozen beauty of embalming. The idea of suicide dawns on him a little later on while he is standing by a shop window with a colourful display of stuffed birds and in that moment it appears to him as the only liberating and redeeming act he can undertake.

Edgardo Limentani seems to be 'yesterday's man', moving through a landscape forever changing and slipping away, a watery, misty flat land, where a trick of the light renders everything insubstantial. Perhaps he's not even yesterday's man — that seems to be the ex-fascist Bellagarta who has moved from politics into becoming a hotelier catering to the nouveaux riches. Limentani is like the heron, a large impractical bird; inedible and not really worth stuffing either. A terribly haunting figure somehow, he evokes other denizens of 'the drowned world' of the European Jews. In *The Heron* there is the same tone as in the work of the East European Jewish/Israeli writer S.Y.Agnon who in puzzling, deeply allusive stories conjured up what cannot be conjured — immense loss, loss on the scale of genocide. FC & RL

'He walked in haste, now at the end of the Via della Resistenza, determined not to glance toward the great lighters and the barges lined up, as they had been that morning, along the bank of the river port. But once he had sensed at his side the presence of these mouse-coloured immobile forms, so immobile that you would think they were resting, rather than on water, on the mucky bed of the river, he couldn't resist the temptation to stop and look at them.

He had seen boats lined up in that way countless times, especially as a boy, in the canal ports of Cesenatico, Cervia, Porto Corsini: in the days of the blissful endless holidays that were the custom then, before the first war and immediately after it. But from these — low, broad, and surmounted, not by vast, gay sails of bright colours, but by pitiful skeletal rigging in which, light and transparent as gauze, lazy shreds of fog lingered — from these there was no extracting any sense of joy, of life, of freedom.' p146

Senso [Senso]

Set against the scarcely discernible backdrop of Italy's war of unification in the latter half of the nineteenth century, *Senso* can be seen as the last act in the drama of an aristocracy in decline, thoroughly contaminated by its connection to a decaying tradition. Far from the upheavals rocking the country at that time, a clandestine love affair develops between an occupying soldier — a sordid German officer stationed in Venice — and a woman of the occupied nation — the Italian Countess Livia. He is handsome and perverse, she is hardened to life in an unhappy marriage, and their relationship is founded on parallel interests: for her it is the opportunity to give herself up to a passion never experienced before, while for him it is the chance to enjoy the easy life of a deserter, financed by his lover's wealth. But their attempt to escape from the world is doomed to failure and its epilogue is a woman's violent vendetta in the face of betrayal.

This story by a self-professed literary outsider — made into a film by Visconti in 1954 — is striking for its stylistic unity, where the Romantic impulse of the nineteenth century is successfully checked by Realism.

In addition to the celebrated novella *Senso* there are five other short stories in this collection. FC

'I was living in virtual solitude. My social circle had already been getting gradually more restricted, because for some time now the noble families of Trentino, opposed to the count's political opinions, had very politely but firmly been keeping their distance. The young people, being fervently nationalistic, unceremoniously avoided us, indeed hated us. Local officials, not knowing how the war would end, and wary of compromising themselves one way or another, now avoided setting foot in our house. So, we were seeing a few pro-Austrian aristocrats, all of them penniless and parasitic, and a few high-ranking Tyrolese officials, who were crass, pig-headed and stank of beer and cheap tobacco. Army officers no longer had any free time to spare, nor any desire to spend it in my company.' p37

An Interview about Old Heaven, New Earth [Vecchio Cielo, Nuova Terra]

Ginevra Bompiani is a new name to English-speaking readers with her book Old Heaven, New Earth *(Boulevard 1995). Born in 1939, which makes her a very young member of the Calvino generation of writers, she shares with him a style that is sometimes philosophical in intent and fantastic in content. She claims affinity with Kafka and Robert Walser but it's very hard to think of any writers in English at all like Bompiani; perhaps Anglo-Saxons are*

still sticking close to realism. Nevertheless Ginevra Bompiani creates a special landscape where the thoughtful can recompose themselves, a landscape created from a potent detachment. Perhaps that detachment comes from her aristocratic background, or because she possesses great intelligence and learning in a culture that chiefly values women for beauty and maternity or perhaps she came to her coolness and considered feeling through personal suffering. In Old Heaven, New Earth *Ginevra Bompiani examines such old-fashioned themes — professional ethics, the refinement or degradation of a person's character in ageing, birth and re-birth, that you realise you've stumbled onto something tremendously modern, a book that could potentially have a resounding influence on the new generation of European writing.*

BABEL: When and *why* did you start writing fiction?

BOMPIANI: J.Rodolfo Wilcock, an Argentinian writer who used to live in Italy, said one writes for nothing less than glory itself. I certainly started off in pursuit of glory, writing a novel at the age of seven and a half. The glory was in the attempt to beat an eight year old English authoress who my father had published with a novel written directly (and approximately) in Italian; her novel was called *The Young Guests.* Mine was called *Because of a Match* and told of the happenings and catastrophes that came from a lit match carelessly discarded... I didn't overtake that very young authoress who kept her lead on me and perhaps I don't write for glory any more, but it still interests me what can arise from some little accidental circumstance, from serendipity if you like.

BABEL: What advantages do you think an Italian writer has?

BOMPIANI: An Italian writer has the advantage of the language. Of course it's not a widespread language like English and yet it has, over English, the creative oscillation between a rich tradition and an impoverished daily usage. There exist such very different cultures, each pulls the language in its own way and happily mangles it. But Italian is a very malleable and resistant language which holds on to its rhythms and has a syntax as pliable as kidskin. Italian swings between two poles, the standardized language used in newspapers, on television, in the supermarket; the language of classroom and bureaucracy (the language of unease) and the dialects (the language of ease), the intimate coves and inlets of the language which still flourish in everyday speech.

BABEL: The story *Enchantment* (in *Old Heaven, New Earth*) seems to create a space and time which exists outside our own age. Your characters move around inside the modern age but in your book there is no sound of machinery, no consumer urging, no nervous pursuit of status.

BOMPIANI: I don't feel that the space of my stories is outside our own age. It's just that our world is difficult to look at as a whole — with the gaze of the eighteenth century writer — because looked at as a whole it reflects an ad-agency, false-tragic vision of its self. Because of that, to really see it I try to look at it out of the corner of my eye. I try to see these aspects, these things that are a bit 'off-stage' that get only the reflected light of the global show. One of these off-stage events is the dramatic situation of the elderly. In reality we're all 'elderly'. The old are the metaphor for us all. They live as we all live; plonked down in front of the television where the global show unreels (massacres, wars, bloodbaths, rapes and refugees...). while our life is all spent within the brief space of the daily round, hedged in by illnesses and detergents. Without the television there wouldn't be a 'world'...

It's not that there's no 'sound of machinery' in my books but that when my characters go down to the street they have to run so as not to be run over; there isn't any anxious consumerism or bridling ambition because these are people seen in the moment in which they stop to ask themselves 'What am I up to? What's happening to me?'

I live in the country so as to be able to hear the world, not to separate myself from it... I try to silence some noises to better hear the sound of those that are less impermanent, harder to hear, the distant rumble of thunder.

BABEL: In the present generation of Italian writers I see a division between those like Sandro Veronese who seem to be writing the Italian version of Anglo-Saxon or International models, as in *Per dove parte questo treno allegro?*, which is a classic *Bildungsroman* (a German model, adopted by the Anglo-Saxons), or Andrea Di Carlo who does something similar in *The Cream Train,* while Pier Vittorio Tondelli does a kind of Jack Kerouac 'Road-story' in *Separate Rooms.* Antonio Tabucchi seems to be an Italian follower of Borges and Gianni Celati reminds me of the early George Orwell.

There also seems to be another strain entirely, a post-Calvino generation of 'Mythical Realists', descendants or anti-descendants of the neo-realists like Tozzi, Pratolini and Pavese who carpet-bombed Italian letters and cinema with their explosive social conscience work in the 40s and early 50s. As 'Magical Realism' in Latin America is supposed to be a way of describing the Surrealism imposed on everyday life by the undigested and indigestible melting pot of Latin American social and cultural reality, Italy seems to have produced a 'Mythical Realist' wave, undoubtedly influenced by the Latin Americans who are even more read in Mediterranean Europe than in the Anglo-Saxon world. Italy has had its own violent Latin Americanesque disjunctures, the exodus from the land to the cities, the near-death of the peasant civilization Pasolini celebrated, the confrontation of venerable provincial societies in Italy's many cities with an International economic and cultural order, all the ideological swings between Extreme Right to Extreme Left with political stagnation at the centre running in parallel with economic dynamism, the poor South versus the rich North etc.

If the reaction of Latin American writers was to try to capture this 'unstable reality' using the 'magical' which can seemingly connect anything with anything in a story then in Italy there is a parallel use of the fabulistic, hence 'Mythical Realism'.

As an example, Elizabetta Rasy writes an essay on the feminine character in a post-Catholic Italy given all the contemporary confusions and stresses by a cod-autobiography of a saint (*La Prima Estasi*), a saint who is constantly in the thrall of weird miracles but who lives in suburbia. Paola Capriolo in *La Grande Eulalia* tells a group of stories set in a world which is distinctly Italian and yet they are about places and personalities that will never be found on a map or in a history book and yet this is not a dream landscape and there is a clear and unmysterious logic to events. Even Valeria Viganò (*Run!*) who evokes contemporary urban reality with quite painful precision draws some of her characters as mythical figures, Antigone and Oedipus for example.

In your work one aspect of this 'Mythical Realism' is that everyday hallucination of Italian life, the presence of the medieval, renaissance, baroque, even the ancient in so many of the cities of Italy. This is a deep peculiarity of Italy, that it is overloaded with its own, (and universal), history. Somewhere in the landscapes and cityscapes of the past, still here in the present, a modern truth is mined, emerging from the disjunctures between contemporary noise and ancient substance.

This leads to the question — do you discover that relationship (between modern existence and all those histories in the Italian countryside and cityscape and civilization) in what you use to write with, does it shape and give birth to your images, to the strange sense of time in your stories?

BOMPIANI: I like the idea of 'mythical realism'; but I wouldn't speak of 'a disjuncture between contemporary noise and ancient substance' because in Italy these two things don't seem disjointed to me, neither are they joined up but let's say they rub up against each other. In any case they're both very much present, as in the rest of Europe (and in Africa and in Asia...), but there's an Italian malleability, a flexibility that isn't solely a matter of the language, and that makes its way between ancient landscapes to the roar of motorbikes with enchantment and insolence...

An event that really strikes me is that meeting between Lawrence Durrell and C.P.Cavafy in Alexandria; Cavafy said to Durrell; 'We Greeks are bankrupt, be careful that the same thing doesn't happen to you English' Well that did happen to us. We've gone bankrupt and we look around in desolation at the marvelous ruins of our inheritance. But along with this astonished gaze at the beauty and the history is also an insolence, something that turns every hole or gully in the country-side into a rubbish dump... Enchantment and insolence are two forms of dependence, two signs of our dependence on beauty and the past, on the fact we are not free of it...

But to go closer to home, this feeling (the relationship to a degraded landscape), seems to me to be at the root of Celati's books, just as the opposite case, the pitiless overabundance of beauty and the misery that accompanies it is found in Anna Maria Ortese's work. What strikes me about the countryside is its potential to detach itself, its sudden appearance, turning a bend in the road, as whole, untouched , silencing every sort of modern existence. The countryside somehow is always *new-born* (as in my story, *Enchantment*) it carries its history on its back as if it were a shirt, as light as a feather, it is a constant *epiphany*...

I believe that the landscape is the part of Italian history to which an Italian writer is most deeply and closely linked (think of that piece by Calvino *From the Opaque* in *Road To San Giovanni*), or even Manganelli describing his death as a land-scape dotted with swamps which one enters on horseback, all the rest — culture, tradition, history of the nation — the Italians are uneasy with, as with the official language. The Italian tradition is the countryside and the dialects.

'It has been the servants who have taken power; not the workers or the slaves or the blacks or the students or the women or the Southerners or the proletariat... Political power .has been taken over by the servants who, after all, were already in place... It is the rule of Harlequin when we hear;

serve, serve the people, the party secretary, serve the Republic, what's meant is serve Harlequin; not to serve without masters, but to serve two masters; yourself and the enemy. That's why we see the politicians come along all hunched up, with memories of every kick in the arse they've taken; and steal from the pantry; and accuse one another while hiding their own hand and at night lie in wait at the street corner to stab you in the side with a kitchen knife; and in the day give themselves a cut of the house-keeping money... They are the descendants of Iago. Loving justice, isn't that the exaggeration of an optimist? (from *Love Sacred & Profane* in *Old Heaven, New Earth*)

BRANCATI
Vitaliano

Bell'Antonio [Il Bell'Antonio]

Written by a Sicilian and set in Sicily, this book tells the bizarre story of Antonio, a young lady-killer whose dashing good looks allow him to exploit to the full the local conventions about male sexual prowess — the idea of the *gallo* (cock). Returning from Rome after a five-year absence, he immerses himself in provincial life and is soon engaged to Barbara, a rich woman captivated by his magnetism. But the outwardly happy marriage soon collapses, revealing to one and all Antonio's misfortune: beneath the polished facade, the great seducer is in fact impotent. The disclosure of his brazen strategy of deceit ostracises him and leaves him without any identity except that of a man who is not 'a real man'. His fall from grace affects his whole family, exposing the vanity and moral bankruptcy of a society founded on an empty ideal of masculine sexual supremacy.

In the novel, Brancati casts a slyly ironic gaze over the phenomenon of sexual conceit known as *gallismo*, which allows the male to establish his dominion over the female by virtue of aggression and power on a sexual level. In this he illustrates the narcissistic vitalism employed to camouflage a profound moral deficiency, the unresolved cultural problem of a society that is incapable of maintaining substantial ethical values. This book strengthens our knowledge of a reality and custom whose survival is more widespread than one might imagine. FC

'That was the most glorious period of my life. I was twenty-four, the women were besotted over me, and I, once a week, was able to make one of them swoon with delight. The very next day began the lies and subterfuges because at all costs I had to avoid going back and sleeping with the lady... How many times I fled to Naples and a hotel on the sea-front, to be tormented by the mandolins outside the restaurants and the smack of kisses from behind closed doors, while I waited for my desire, spread so evenly throughout my body as to seep placidly from my hand whenever I shook that of a woman, to condense into the place which is made for it.... I have never mentioned these things to anyone, but I've written them down and copied them countless times on sheets of paper which I then burnt: by now I know them by heart.' p151

The Lost Years [Gli Anni Perduti]

Brancati was a disillusioned Sicilian fascist when he came to write *The Lost Years*, which was first published (in a rapidly suppressed magazine) at the height of the fascist era in 1938. The 'lost years' are the years of youth and hope, squandered in the inert atmosphere of a town like the one he calls 'Natacà' in provincial Sicily. The major problem for the young people of Natacà is how to wile away the day, how to pass the evening (stay in bed, hang around, hang around some more...). Brancati's genius lies in transforming the leaden boredom that often afflicts adolescence into an entertaining and ironic work of art that is often wildly amusing. It's not just 1930s Sicily that is caught on the skewer: the digestive recourses of small town life — menfolk lying supine beneath the weight of their bellies, waiting for their massive bulk 'to exhale its legs of pork, its wines, its farinaceous foods, and once more become light and portable'— might seem familiar wherever people who gather round tables have more facility for plate-clearing than conversation.

More seriously, the book is also a document of the social and moral atmosphere of Italy under fascism, a document of *everyday* fascism that illustrates how little compromises eventually add up to big, bloody ones. As one character puts it, people 'jettison morality like ballast' when they realise the boat is sinking: 'The first law of morality is to live. The second is to win. The third is to obey the law of morality.'

At the centre of the book is the construction of a marvellous tower from which to view the surrounding landscape: a monument which will, the locals hope, put Natacà on the map, bringing trade and progress and washing out the boredom and inertia that is stifling the town. What actually becomes of this project in 'the country of hitches and delays' you must read for yourself, but be sure that somehow Natacà still didn't much change, nor did its people become much wiser. RL

'Prone in bed in the dark is the most felicitous position for killing time, now letting your eyes close, now lending an ear to the street noises, now to the flies hunting daylight at the crack between the shutters; sometimes nodding off, at others thinking thoughts that could be easily the hem of a dream, you slip from eight to eleven — hey presto! In a jiffy.'p30

BUFALINO
Gesualdo

Night's Lies [Le Menzonge Della Notte]

Night's Lies is a historical novel that deals with the lives and adventures of revolutionaries in an age of conspirators and *Carbonari* (Eighteenth-century revolutionaries), a world of vast political and intellectual agitation. The principal character is a 'God-fearing sanguinary brigand' who has lived on the run for forty years, wreaking havoc across the countryside. Not your average eighteenth-century crook or footpad, he is said to be 'of vast intelligence' and, while looting monasteries and country houses, will 'ransack the library for books to read.'

Perhaps the novel doesn't quite carry off its rhetorical code of 'ye olde'-speak. It is, however, full of striking images of an existence infinitely strange and yet still familiar to us, like the seminary in which a young orphan is brought up — a male, black-clad world in which the older orphans serve as adults for the younger ones.

If the literary or linguistic style is a sub-archaic torture of modern prose, the question becomes; is it entertaining, creatively benign and even evocative, or is it just silly and tiresome? RL

'The storm had blown itself out. As if hacked into a hundred pieces by the swish of a gigantic sabre, the cowling of black clouds permitted slats to reappear here and there between the shreds. Mingling with the succulent damp of the soil, the air grew sultry. One last rumble of thunder, deprived of vehemence, like the growl of a well-fed mastiff, was heard fading away far out over the water, where sea and sky raised a single barbican of darkness.' p90

Plague-Sower [Diceria del Untore]

By transferring the exquisitely Nordic atmosphere of the sanitorium into a Sicily of baroque radiance and gleaming seas Bufalino perhaps meant to place his story of sickness and death within the tradition of the nineteenth century novel. In fact it's 1946, the war is over, but up in the mountains; 'Mount Athos, the fortress of La Rochelle, Ucciardone prison... there were so many enclosures and solitary retreats to which I liked to compare our situation at La Rocca. Nor did I forget the castle of Atlante. That is, a place of visions destined not to last. Marta was one such vision.'

In this place of visions the narrator has a vision of his own which is not destined to endure either; his love story with Marta. She is an ex-ballerina with a troubled and mysterious past, laden with misfortune. He becomes influenced by the destructive vein within her which longs for catharsis but equally she excises 'that weakness of the heart which wants to learn to die', leaving him in the end with a little strength for himself.

With a highly developed control over his language Bufalino reveals the 'writing self', releasing it from behind the protective wall where he felt as a young man he would always belong. He evokes a landscape, a time and place both private and shared which seems to live again between the countryside and the sea. His choice of words is always erudite and dignified, like a perfectly-aimed arrow never missing its target. FC

'Usually I have little tolerance for those who recount their dreams even though I so often fall prey to the same vice. But with her it was different, and I listened to her lovingly. She was as though raving at my side, tale-bearer of some hereafter, sprinkling her long delirium with a string of catchy, contrived monologues of the sort that we love so much to hear in popular songs and the lamentations of poets. Shavings, her speeches were, shavings of pinchbeck, a moulting plumage, a fine dust of seed pearls and trifles belonging to a dethroned queen of hearts, beneath which one glimpsed — just barely, but it was there — the implacable bone of death. Which I wanted to reach, having no other means, with the curious sword of sex...' p107

Seminar On Youth [Seminario sulla Gioventù],

The Standard Life Of A Pantyhose Salesman [Vita standard di un venditore provvisorio di collant],

Sodomies In Eleven Point [Sodomie in Corpo II]

'My career is to become 'Me', I can no longer be content with anything less,' writes Aldo Busi. In a sense, he has achieved this aim and become a twentieth-century *agent provocateur*, in the tradition of Sade and Nietzsche. While his early novels *Seminar on Youth* and *Standard Life of a Pantyhose Salesman* are fictional representations of a larger-than-life existence, *Sodomies in Eleven Point* is a personal sounding-off. Here, Busi decadently raps and wriggles his way through the great themes of literature and homosexuality, casually dismissing his predecessors. Gide, Genet and Pasolini are called apologists and Moravia a 'bourgeois pornographer'. He scoffs at travelogues and books about sex, but then, tongue-in-cheek, hurtles his reader into a torrid sexual exploration of North Africa, Finland and Czechoslovakia.

Outside his books Busi actively lives up to his reputation as a 'literary Cicciolina' (Italy's onetime 'Queen of Porn'). He appeared naked at the launch of *Standard Life* and was almost prosecuted for obscenity for *Sodomies in Eleven Point*, something that caused sales of the book to rocket. Many Italian writers, elbowed out of the literary circus of parties and conferences by the more glamorous Busi, are angry. But this 'starlet' status belies some rather sharp writing, or 'acid aperçus' as Philip Hensher remarked in *The Guardian*. Take, for instance, the superb and much-quoted one-liner: 'Eroticism is the candied cherry on the cake when the cake is missing'.

'In dissenting, one speaks,' writes Busi in his last book. Substitute 'writes' for 'speaks' and you have the essence of Busi. *Seminar On Youth*, his first novel, tells of Barbino's mutation from child hip-shaking mambo dancer to young man gratifying the needs of the village youths and, finally, to prostitute in Milan and Paris. Barbino's sexual encounters with men are often violent and complicated. He is locked in a cupboard for three days, drawn into a sado-masochistic relationship with a rich art dealer, abused by a grouchy old Parisian and his two Arab sidekicks. But on each occasion Barbino's tenacity and ingenuity provide the escape route.

Like *Seminar*, *Standard Life* focuses on a fervid young man who is searching for another way of life, trying to forge his own 'moral' code in a quest for personal identity. But identity, Busi points out, is a curious thing: if culture is identity then why can't we change our identity by moving to Paris?

Both Barbino and Angelo are 'marginalised' by being homosexuals but turn their homosexuality into a vibrant and aggressive exhortation of sex. If the traditional stereotype of the homosexual is 'someone who desires incessantly', Busi is candidly matter-of-fact about his own promiscuity. 'I do not make love because I like it, but because I do not know what else to do'. This 'accountancy of the heart' is the backdrop to his novels. Angelo, part-time literary translator and interpreter for pantyhose salesman Celestino Lometto, cruises around Europe looking for sex in bars and public toilets and on the banks of Lake Garda. *Sodomies in Eleven Point* chronicles Busi's numerous, usually paid-for and often violent sexual encounters. A literary seminar in Finland leaves him sulky and melancholy as he cannot fathom the country's complete lack of sexual opportunity.

Busi's sexuality reflects a two-fold aim in life: '1. to take part at all costs, 2. to set myself apart by choice'. In Barbino and Angelo he explores these possibilities. Barbino's strategy is a paradoxical marriage of violence and pacifism 'to acquire good aim through practice massacres and never to have to fire a single shot'. He strives to unearth people's motives and the ties that bind them in strange relationships. What truths, for instance, do prim Nougatine and the despicable colonel conceal? And what subtleties underlie the friendship between timid Arlette, aloof careerist Genevieve and the maternal Suzanne? Ultimately, Barbino and Angelo act as subversive catalysts. 'To invade a person's existence with my presence, making and unmaking its existence, almost always changing him into one who no longer knows who he is when I take my leave because I never reveal the code word to break the spell'.

Busi's writing reflects this same push and pull of assertion and withdrawal. He indulges in some wonderfully humorous character sketches: Clementina Gnoccoli, heiress of an underwear empire; pill-popping matriarch Edna Lometto, married to a pantyhose empire; even his mother's domestic economy, knitting on a bench under a street-lamp to save electricity, is brilliantly set up. But all of it goes nowhere — probably because Busi is astute enough to realise a basic tenet: 'To attack the platitudes of the world means to remove from beneath it the only piles on which it rests — with this difference, that it doesn't notice and you are the only one to collapse underneath it'.

Suffering is something so quiet and understated in Busi's writing that it is easily overlooked, perhaps because the suffering that ostracizes Busi and his protagonists leads them to pluck up their heels and stamp them firmly one step in front. Suffering, in any case, is, according to Busi, ephemeral. For 'what remains of the pain we thought we suffered when we were young? Nothing'. It serves no purpose, in actual fact, as 'in pieces or in one piece, don't we go on living equally split?'

Busi is throwing up all the cards and slamming the door before they land. Despite his pooh-poohing of the Italian literary giants, he remains quintessentially Italian. All his references come from the innards of his Brescian landscape, even Finland — 'hundreds of kilometres of Lombardy before the discovery of fire and the invention of the wheel'. Busi is like Voltaire's Candide, haphazardly stabbing his fork into a Utopian ideal, though this *enfant terrible* is probably far from ready to cultivate his garden. HB

'Here I am in Milan again, looking for a little luck, like so many others as thwarted as myself....But it will not be for long; if I have to pick up lice they might as well be Parisian lice.

I am working at the very exclusive Bar Pinguino in Via Verri, I am a waiter, or rather I go round the shops and beauty-parlours carrying through the traffic trays piled with ices with their little paper umbrellas and martinis with glacé cherries in them. I have found lodgings just a step away, in Via Bigli, in a ramshackle attic belonging to a tailor: a camp-bed there was already, and with a bit here and bit there I have managed to put together a bed. Hundreds of beetles about — they don't even wait for the dark; I don't even squash them. There are so many of them that they squash each other I imagine. Now one is peeping out from this page, who knows what it is trying to say to me.' p118 *Seminar on Youth*

The Tartar Steppe [Il Deserto Dei Tartari]

This is the story of a young officer, Lieutenant Giovanni Drogo, who is sent on his first commission to Fort Bastiani, a desert outpost which is supposedly a vital strategic buffer against enemy attack. He reaches it with an enormous sense of relief and it seems at first that his stay there will provide the existential opportunity that he's long been waiting for. 'It was the day he'd been awaiting for years, the beginning of his real life'. But once there, Drogo is involved in a new and unnerving period of waiting, uninterrupted by either enemy assault or, indeed, any sign of life whatsoever. Ironically, the long-awaited chance of a heroic act that would instill some meaning in Drogo's spiritually empty life arises only at the moment when he is no longer capable of discharging it, as illness and death prevent him from finally confronting the enemy and redeeming a long, immobile existence bereft of any real achievement.

In an atmosphere reminiscent of Kafka's *The Castle*, Buzzati creates a symbolic interior voyage in search of an existential alternative that would allow a man to become himself through an authentic relationship with action. That his flight from a mediocre and lifeless reality towards the unknown ends up in another defeat reveals that an individual's room for manoeuvre counts as nothing against the power of a cruel destiny.

Buzzati himself said of the book that made him famous: 'I ought to have spent my whole life writing this book, or at least into late middle age, because it's really a kind of autobiography'. It is the uncompletable work that tells the story of a writer's impossible adventure in his writing. FC

'His talk with the general down in the city had left him with few hopes of a transfer and a brilliant career, but Giovanni knew he could not stay within the walls of the Fort all his life. Sooner or later he would have to make up his mind. Then the old habits caught him up again with the old rhythm and Drogo no longer thought of the others, of the comrades who had escaped in time, of his old friends grown rich and famous; he consoled himself with the sight of the officers who shared his exile; it never occurred to him that they might be the weak ones, the ones who had been beaten, the last people to take as an example.' p165

Restless Nights [Le Notti Difficili]

Buzzati's nights, surreal places, are certain both to delight and dismay the reader. We meet monsters and witness miracles, but a constant rhythm runs throughout, a recognisable backdrop of facts and clues that allude to and resemble the entire maelstrom of collective existence. Like fables but lacking any moralistic aim, these stories, spawned by Buzzati's dedication to fantasy and invention which he held as essential to freedom, are intended to give everyone the chance to dream. Their ironies and paradoxes momentarily break the ties that keep us social animals earthbound, and we are seduced by the idea of a fourth dimension in which everyone's existence turns into dreamlike fantasy. This is the case with *The Count's Wife*, which recounts one woman's Kafkaesque metamorphosis as a way of escaping the drabness of provincial life, or *The Scandal on Via Sesostri*, in which one man's death reveals his true identity and at the same time the false identity of us all.

What stands out in each story is Buzzati's journalistic interpretation of the dreamworld, which captures a sphere of visions and apparitions in the detached manner of news commentary. In this sense he maintains a close and vital link with reality, the aim of each story being to expose the social pretence which debases people, killing the individual while allowing only a licensed existence. FC

'One morning about ten o'clock an immense fist appeared in the sky above the city. Then it slowly unclenched and remained this way, immobile, like an enormous canopy of ruin. It looked like rock, but it was not rock; it looked like flesh but it wasn't; it even seemed made of cloud, but cloud it was not. It was God, and the end of the world.' p7

A Love Affair [Un Amore]

Love surprises the staid, middle-aged protagonist of the novel on a visit to a brothel. This illicit passion is aroused by the dazzle of youth, this unexpected and unfamiliar emotion provoked by the sight of the beautiful prostitute Laide, a woman who is only apparently within his reach. What is merely a game for her, to be played with cynical unscrupulousness, becomes an obsession for him, a continual source of jealousy and anxiety onto which all his existential terrors are projected. Surrounding them is Milan, a corrupt city, an ungovernable

Babel, a secret and indecipherable labyrinth as confusing as Laide. Woman and city merge in an indefinable mystery, both symptoms of the world-weariness which torments the book's main character. There is no redemption in this love, therefore, no regeneration: eroticism is the only sphere accessible to a man who has too long refused to face his own emotions. All the same, it's eroticism which provides a final glimmer of hope in Laide's alleged pregnancy which, if it breaks the spell of the mystery surrounding her, could introduce her to the everyday emotions of normal life.

Written in the 1960s, *A Love Affair* is atypical of Buzzati's work: here, all the standard features of his prose and subject matter are abandoned, and in this sense it's a unique text where, as the writer Guido Piovene rightly said, 'the surreal is supplanted by the real'. FC

'He day-dreamed that Laide had fallen under a street car and lost a leg. How wonderful that would be! Deformed, cut off forever from the world of prostitution, and dancing and sexual adventures, she would no longer be at the mercy of all those people. Only Antonio would continue to worship her. And that might be his only hope that Laide, if for no other reason than gratitude, would begin to love him... She was the symbol of a world that was common and nocturnal, gay and vicious, fearlessly wicked and sure of itself, a world that teemed with life insatiable, surrounded by the boredom and respectability of the middle class.' p92

CALASSO
Roberto

The Marriage Of Cadmus And Harmony [Le Nozze Di Cadmus E Armonia]

Roberto Calasso is the editorial director of the respected Milan publishing house Adelphi Edizioni and a well-known intellectual and literary figure both in Italy and abroad. He has been nicknamed 'l'anti-Eco' — the 'anti-Umberto Eco' — by the Italian press. *The Marriage Of Cadmus And Harmony* is his third and most successful book; it was a bestseller in Italy, won the 1991 Prix Veillon and the 1992 Prix de Meilleur Livre Étranger in France and has been fêted in America by Susan Sontag and Gore Vidal among others.

Indeed, Vidal says that it belongs alongside the Old and New Testaments as a text it is necessary to know in order to understand Western civilisation. Such a claim is certainly not provoked simply by Calasso's subject matter, namely classical Greek myths and Homeric tales, but equally by the fact that his book is not so much *about* these as a brilliant re-creation of them. Although they incorporate immense scholarship, there is nothing antiquarian or detached about these stories. They are extraordinarily fresh and vivid, both as stories and in the accompanying interpretative asides.

These asides are contemporary without being anachronistic. From the Odyssey, for example, Calasso derives the moral that fortune's slings and arrows are sent to test us and that 'the sovereignty of the mind lies in recognising, in dealing with them as such, in getting through with the secretly indifferent curiosity of the traveller.' Again: his analysis of the genealogy of modern totalitarianism begins with Sparta — the first instance in which 'the group of initiates becomes the police force.' Calasso avoids anachronism because he makes no concessions to modern prudishness, squeamishness or soft-centred psychologising. Indeed, these tales may be 'foundational' for us as much for their undisguised violence, murder, pillage, rape, erotic mayhem and sacrifice (both human and animal) as anything else.

Yet there are also moments of great tenderness and grace. Calasso notes that for the ancient Greeks 'Every sudden heightening of intensity brought you into a god's sphere of influence.' Insofar as whatever most moved them still moves us — whether because of a shared humanity or cultural ancestry or both — this element can be found in these rich, contradictory tales of the gods and goddesses and their human peers, bearing out Calasso's claim that all modern civilisation has done is 'invent, for the powers that act upon us, longer, more numerous, more awkward names, which are less effective...'

He is not afraid to intervene and compare ancients and moderns, pointing out, for example, that while modern atheists believe they control their lives, Homer's heroes felt themselves 'being sustained and imbued by something remote and whole, which abandoned them at death like so many rags' — and he does so in such a way that the attitude of the ancients feels at least as fresh and accessible.

There are many other points to savour: the revealing of the

enmity between Homer and Plato, for example — truer and deeper than between the latter and Aristotle or even the followers of Christ. And it is a wonderful paradox that Calasso has produced such an elegant and rational argument against the Enlightenment that bequeathed him its very style and (in a sense) spirit. But then, as he shows, even the chief weapons against myth are themselves mythical: the capacity for objectivity, control and domination is Athena's, and 'when it first came into being, system itself was no more than a flap on a god's cloak, a minor bequest of Apollo.' PC

'...when something undefined and powerful shakes mind and fibre and trembles the cage of our bones, when the person who only a moment before was dull and agnostic is suddenly rocked by laughter and homicidal frenzy, or by the pangs of love, or by the hallucination of form, or finds his face streaming with tears, then the Greek realises that he is not alone. Somebody else stands beside him, and that somebody is a god.'

CALVINO
Italo

If On A Winter's Night A Traveller [Se un notte d'inverno un viaggiatore]

A book about books about writing about reading; maybe a modernist masterpiece, Calvino being (in 1979) far ahead of his time once again. This work is an extended reflection, like *The Cloven Viscount* and (in a different way) *Italian Folk Tales*, on the way narrative itself works. The structure of *If On A Winter's Night...* follows that of mirrors reflecting into other mirrors, so we have a story that feeds on itself and mutates into a different story (or is it a different storyteller?) every ten or twenty pages. It's a virtuoso piece — but one that, unusually, reveals rather than conceals its workings.

What happens in the book is rather beyond description as it is the 'happeningness' of books that happens here — but for sure amongst the unfoldings of this twisted tale are a whole series of true and witty reflections. In deciding not to describe a female character's home, for example, the narrator explains that the reader could probably list all its contents without even looking, so uniform and prescriptive is our civilisation. This is one of the things that makes Calvino worth reading: his incisive take on the consumer society — something that flowered, if that is the word, in Italy at the same time as he matured as a writer. Nobody does it better. Another thing to love him for is his humour, here describing what *really* happens when someone goes into a bookshop: RL

'...you have forced your way through the shop past the thick barricade of Books You Haven't Read, which were frowning at you from the tables and shelves, trying to cow you. But you know you must never allow yourself to be awed, that among them there extend for acres the Books You Needn't Read, Books Made For Purposes Other Than Reading, Books Read Even Before You Open Them Since They Belong To The Category Of Books Read Before Being Written.' p10

Invisible Cities [Le Città Invisibili]

Invisible Cities is a kind of *I Ching* or book of wisdom and commentary for the modern age. One of Calvino's last books, it consists of fifty-five brief chapters, each of which describes a different imaginary city. The cities are at once mysterious and vaguely allegorical, reflecting various aspects and conditions of modern urban life.

In the 'continuous city' of Cecilia, for example, a wanderer encounters a goatherd who despises all cities — for him they are just criminal interruptions of good pasture — hurrying his flock away from town. Years later the two men meet again, but this time the goatherd is wizened, his goats so reduced that 'they did not even stink'. He explains that Cecilia has become inescapable as all the cities in the world have joined together across all the pasture lands in the world, forcing his goats to graze on traffic islands.

The marvelous city of *Zora*, on the other hand, is remote, lying 'beyond six rivers and three mountain ranges'. The learned travel there because, forever kept unchanging, it serves as a giant mnemonic or remembering machine. Retained in the memory, its details (the fountain with the nine jets, the barber's striped awning, the statue of the hermit and the lion) can be substituted by the details of any science or philosophy; its structure forms a giant periodic table for any branch of knowledge, whether the elements of this branch are music, dentistry or theology.

In this respect of course Zora is the antithesis of London or Tokyo or New York, where history and memory are daily ground under the earth-hammers of property developers. But then so gentle is Calvino's touch that it can be read either as a critique of such development or as advocating it: forced to remain motionless and always the same, Zora has 'languished, disintegrated and disappeared' from the face of the earth.

The last of Calvino's cities is 'Berenice the unjust', whose corrupt patricians at the baths 'observe with a proprietary eye the round flesh of the bathing odalisques' while, down in the city's cellars, their opponents, who nourish themselves on a 'sober but tasty cuisine' based on grains and pulses, prepare for the reign of justice. Unfortunately, alongside their thirst for justice they are nurturing a malignant seed in their breasts: 'the certainty and pride of being in the right'. And Calvino urges us to 'peer deeper into this new germ of justice and discern...the mounting tendency to impose what is just through what is unjust.' An excellent suggestion in a world beset by opposing, sometimes well-armed, self-righteous political, ethnic and religious groupings. RL

"'I have also thought of a model city from which I deduce all the others," Marco answered. "It is a city made only of exceptions, exclusions, incongruities, contradictions. If such a city is the most improbable, by reducing the number of elements we increase the probability that the city really exists. So I have only to subtract exceptions from my model, and in whatever direction I proceed, I will arrive at one of the cities which, always as an exception, exist. But I cannot force my operation beyond a certain limit: I would achieve cities too probable to be real.'" p56

Marcovaldo, or The Seasons In The City [Marcovaldo]

This is one of Calvino's chronicles of a changing Italy. Marcovaldo is a Candide-like naïf observer of urban life. He has the heart of a countryman but, to make a living, has to live in an ugly and polluted Northern city. In a gentle, humorous way, Calvino points out how the cities created or expanded by the economic boom years are uncomfortable, grubby and short of open space.

It takes an extraordinarily light touch to be able to tell this story and make the reader smile at the same time. Amongst the best of the twenty little episodes that make up *Marcovaldo* are *The Garden of Stubborn Cats*, *The Wasp Treatment* and the adventures of *The Poisonous Rabbit*. Although one of Calvino's most accessible books — in fact, a book a child might enjoy — it is neither a conventional short story collection, nor a novel, nor a novella. As in *Invisible Cities*, Calvino here takes a format from early medieval writing to use in his own (very) contemporary way. RL

'It was a time when the simplest foods contained threats, traps, and frauds. Not a day went by without some newspaper telling of ghastly discoveries in the housewife's shopping: cheese was made of plastic, butter from tallow candles; in fruit and vegetables the arsenic of insecticides was concentrated in percentages higher than the vitamin content; to fatten chickens they stuffed them with synthetic pills that could transform the man who ate a drumstick into a chicken himself. Fresh fish had been caught the previous year in Iceland and they put make-up on the eyes to make it seem yesterday's catch. Mice had been found in several milk-bottles, whether dead or alive was not made clear. From the tins of oil it was no longer the golden juice of the olive that flowed, but the fat of old mules, cleverly distilled.' p67

The Road to San Giovanni [La Strada di San Giovanni]

One of several posthumously-published works of Calvino (who died in 1985), that were assembled from unfinished manuscripts, *Road To San Giovanni* collects various autobiographical pieces. There's his account of his early love-affair with film, (*A Cinema-Goer's Autobiography*) with him sneaking off every afternoon in the provincial town of his youth to be immersed in flickering dreams; an episode from WWII fighting in Italy (*Memories of a Battle*) as well as his more contemporary struggle to take out the garbage from his Paris flat (*La Poubelle agréée*).

As this is work that the writer himself didn't see as ready for publication the collection is uneven, there is the sense of ideas not quite digested, stories not quite yet fully written. In a way though this shows off Calvino's abilities all the better; seeing his work as if stripped down to a rawer stage the 'effortless' lightness of his polished and completed stories can be seen as the fine, skillful artefacts that they are.

The main justification for this book though is the title story; a long and close description of his father's life and way of being, recollected or reconstructed by a son over many years. On first reading it is merely delightful as Calvino conjures up an environment of market gardens and terraces amidst the fertile and welcoming nature of Liguria. On reflection though it becomes a marvellous statement about the maturing of the relation between parent and child; in particular the strange fact that we can never understand our parents *at the time* because their lives and experiences always run a full generation ahead of ours. *The Road to San Giovanni* has the middle-aged writer remembering and retrospectively admiring his agriculturist father and realising the similarities between them, one a cultivator of seeds, the other of words, affinities that apparent differences of taste hid during his youth.

Anyone who has wondered about the mysterious link between parent and child will find this a very rewarding piece. RL

'The face of Jean Gabin was made of different stuff, physiologically and psychologically, from the faces of those American actors, faces that would never look up from a table bespattered with soup and humiliation as at the beginning of *La Bandera*....French cinema was as heavy with smells as American films were light with Palmolive, polish and antiseptic. The women had a carnal presence that established them in the film-goer's mind as at once living women and erotic fantasies...while the eroticism of the Hollywood stars was sublimated, stylized, idealized.'
A Cinema-Goer's Autobiography p49

Under The Jaguar Sun [Sotto il Sole Giaguaro]

A short unfinished work but nevertheless a fabulous descent into the world of the senses. This book comes from the period when Calvino was such an established artist that he could experiment and still command an audience. As with *Invisible Cities*, this is the kind of writing, neither realist nor surreal, neither wholly narrative nor straightforward exposition, that points to the future of the written word.

The first and title story of the three pieces in *Under The Jaguar Sun* shows a couple communicating with each other by sharing the passionate, exotic tastes of Mexican cuisine, in which two continents' worth of foodstuffs and culinary which two continents' worth of foodstuffs and culinary traditions meet and clash. Calvino's clever narration darts between sex and food, whipping the reader up into a fine old state — as it does this couple who travel around Mexico, seemingly trying to devour the whole country. This short but blazing piece manages to be a celebration of so many things: a couple's complicity with each other, the sensuality of eating, seriously engaged travelling...

The middle story, *A King Listens*, is an ironic piece about dictatorship, appearances, resistance. The last story, *The Name, The Nose*, is a perfect salad of bad taste and exquisiteness, a serious meditation on the sense of smell (Calvino's plan was for a book on the five senses). A narrative that interweaves three parallel stories, it is led by the adventures of Monsieur de Sainte-Caliste, a Parisian gentleman of the nineteenth century who runs an account at Madame Odile's, a leading parfumerie of the city. RL

'And one of her shopgirls, Martine, was already tickling the tip of my ear with her finger wet with patchouli (pressing the sting of her breast, at the same time, beneath my armpit), and Charlotte was extending her arm, perfumed with orris, for me to sniff (in the same fashion, on other occasions, I had examined a whole sampler, arrayed over her body), and Sidonie blew on my hand, to evaporate the drop of eglantine she had put there (between her parted lips I could glimpse her little teeth, whose bites I knew so well), and another, whom I had never seen, a new girl (whom I merely grazed with an absent pinch, preoccupied as I was), aimed an atomizer at me, pressing its bulb, as if inviting me to an amorous skirmish.'
p69

The Watcher/La Giornata d'uno Scrutatore, La Nuvola di Smog, La Formica Argentina

A fairly early work that uncannily captures the atmosphere of a rapidly industrialising, modernising Northern Italy in the late 1950s. Calvino's genius as a writer is to travel beyond the satirical (stereotyped clerks and advertising men) into a convincingly acidulous vision of a city all shine and sparkle on the outside but simultaneously pervaded by dirt and unease.

To accomplish the writerly mission of capturing the world

afresh he adopts the technique of looking through the eyes of impossibly innocent creatures. In the story *Smog*, the clerk who works for the Air Pollution Institute (controlled by industrialists busy poisoning the atmosphere) is shown an illustrated propaganda magazine about Soviet life by a communist acquaintance and sees only 'An Asiatic race, with fur caps and boots, blissfully going to fish in a river.' This Arcadian vision of Soviet Central Asia under Stalin — in reality a hell of forced industrialisation, nuclear testing and political tyranny — is presented in a way that mixes the character's faux-naiveté with the writer's ruthless irony: 'I had been looking,' the clerk tells us, 'for a new image of the world which would give meaning to our grayness, which would compensate for all the beauty that we were losing...'

In *The Watcher* the naive eye is turned onto politics and sees election posters, one pasted over the other in 'a patina of paste and cheap paper, where, layer upon layer, the symbols of the opposing parties could be read, transparently.' An effective image of Italian politics where a plethora of parties, financed out of the public purse, use these funds to cover with meaningless slogans the walls of every village in the land, which finally merge into an indistinguishable mess of paper particles and garish party symbols. A attack on a corrupt system that like the story *Smog*, is full of foresight.

The Watcher is a story about the morality of politics and about political duty in the widest sense. An election scrutineer visits a huge 'home for unfortunates', the Cottolengo Hospital in Turin and longs for his mistress. A sign of a great writer might be how he or she lures us unwittingly into new and uncomfortable thoughts, as here where Calvino sets up a wicked contrast between the sad drabs of Cottolengo and the girl who is his lover. RL

'Resigned to spending the whole day amongst these drab, colourless creatures, A. felt a yearning for beauty, which became focused in the thought of his mistress, Lia. And what he remembered of Lia was her skin, her colour, and above all one point of her body — where her back arched, distinct and taut, to be caressed with the hand, and then the gentle, swelling curve of the hips — a point where he now felt the world's beauty was concentrated, remote, lost.' p21

CAMON
Ferdinando
The Fifth Estate/Il Quinto Stato

The 'Fifth Estate' are the peasantry and this is a tour-de-force narrative of peasant existence. The story told is in itself definitely interesting, with all the usual set pieces; such as the reduction of the treasured family hog into prosciutto and pork chops; the traumas of village idiots and the wars of country youth for possession of the neighbouring *fanciulle brave* or local lookers.

As a piece of writing it is also of great interest because it shows that stream-of-consciousness and almost completely unpunctuated narrative can be completely readable and engaging. Camon says he wrote *Fifth Estate* this piece in a burst of evenings and Sunday mornings snatched from the round of domestic existence.

Perhaps it is the sincerity of the writer that goes to the heart, Camon himself comes from the (almost completely vanished) world he describes; 'Having been born in its midst I was soaked through with its grandiose and wretched, heroic and humiliating myths, like a sponge in a pail...' and he laments its passing. In any case here are all the best stories of peasant life told one rolling into another, comprising a thrilling literary achievement, translated and successful all around the world. RL

'when an ox breaks its chain the woman who's left at home bolts the gate and rushes off by bicycle to the fields to tell her husband yelling all the way at the top of her lungs King's got loose or Giant, Spaniard's got loose or Paintbrush, Old Three Hundred's got loose, everybody in the village knows that Giant is harmless but rambunctious and when he doesn't get away it's simply because he's satisfied with the alfalfa you've given him real alfalfa and not wheat straw the Brucacasdottis are so stingy that they often give their oxen yellow straw to eat and put special green glasses on them so they'll think it's green grass...' p54

For Love, Only For Love/Per Amore, Solo Per Amore

This is the biblical story of Mary and Joseph transplanted into the real world where people fall in love, get married, fall out of love etc.. Joseph is portrayed as a bit of a man about town, liked by all the young women and given to occasional flirting with them. He first meets Mary as a young girl, and it's only later that he wins her hand. The story is narrated mostly by Joseph's servant, who describes the attraction his master holds for the women of the village, his eventual betrothal to Mary despite the attentions of older mistresses, and then his rage when he discovers that she's pregnant despite the fact that their marriage has never been consummated. Joseph stays with Mary and helps her bring up their son, and eventually dies, still in the dark about the secret of Jesus' birth.

Readers are placed in an ironic position since they have foreknowledge of the story and, therefore, the overview that Joseph lacks. But the book does tell a well-known story in a different way, fleshing it out with realistic details. Jesus is portrayed as a normal son who is nevertheless very intelligent and already shows a predilection for looking after the outcast, the poor and the sick. Joseph treats him like any father would and occasionally they argue, since Jesus is quite rebellious, Joseph getting angry at Mary for taking their son's side as it undermines his authority.

This is definitely an interesting picture of life in a less familiar part of the ancient world, but emotionally it is clearly a glamourised version of Italian provincial life, the lads and lasses growing up, messing around but then settling down and having bambinos and so forth.

For Love, Only for Love is written with a charming, Italianate, sympathy for youth and childhood which removes the stiffness of the historical novel. Campanile propels his colourful barque with just the right amount of exotic puff in its sails. LR + RL

'Phoenicians wearing embroidered trousers under their tunics...men with goatskin cloaks coming from the plains of Anatolia... Some ladies, to indicate their position as married women, denied the approach of any man other than their husband, wore a short golden chain linking their ankles, and walked in tiny steps...' p49

CARDELLA
Lara

Good Girls Don't Wear Trousers [Volevo I Pantaloni]

Lara Cardella, a writer born in 1969, describes here a present-day Italy stuck in the Middle Ages, characterised by the violence and abuse of an apparently everyday Southern Italian family. The protagonist and narrator, Anna, is a Sicilian teen-ager who finds herself unable to conform to the traditional role of submissive female and is forced to steal a false freedom for herself with lipsticks and miniskirts. The trousers she longs for are a symbol of the independence enjoyed only by men in a culture of continual discrimination against the female sex. Her early attempts to be male, imitating stereotypical masculine behaviour, are the first steps on the long road towards her goal of reclaiming herself and her own individuality. But the impossibility of transforming herself into the triumphant image of her own oppressor forces her to the opposite extreme: the most reviled role of the *buttana* (whore). This book became quite a literary *cause celebre* not only because its author was only eighteen but also because it reveals that the Southern tradition of bringing up girls in an atmosphere of coercion and self-negation is continuing in a society where modernisation and emancipation from the past have left whole areas of life still in the shadows. FC

CARLO
Andrea di

The Cream Train [Il Treno di Panna]

Giovanni, a twenty-five year old Italian, arrives in Los Angeles in search of his future. Like the camera he carries around with him, the story takes reels of snapshots of the vacuous lives of the young Californians he meets. From struggling scriptwriter Ron and his ambitious girlfriend Tracy to Jill, the neurotic check-out girl at the Italian restaurant still mourning the departure of her Crooner boyfriend Ray, everyone is chasing the American dream of fame and money. Giovanni skirts through this surreal landscape, De Carlo's camera-like narrative zooming in here and there to give the reader colour-sharp details and in fact before writing this novel De Carlo tried to express himself through photography. The plot is clinically narrated from the outside, although this detachment hints at an underlying layer of moral bankruptcy and despair. HB

'Ron and Tracy were like two young sharks, insecure, quarrelsome, frantic every time the phone rang. They were always on their guard, wary of giving themselves away or of appearing naïve. They saw Los Angeles as an obstacle race, every jump as the latest of a series; they subdivided the endless series of jumps so as to come down to categories and sub-categories. They circled around in search of scraps of success to snap up so as to grow into bigger young sharks...At some moments of total frenzy the telephone numbers on their note-pads were insufficient to sate their craving for opportunities or cues for them to step into the limelight or make themselves known in some way.' p25

CAVAZZONI
Ermanno

The Voice of the Moon [Poema dei Lunatici]

An extended joke — an Idiot-Candide wanders through a boggy version of Northern Italy having his leg extensively pulled by a succession of the kind of village wise guys who haunt provincial bars. The faux-naif narrator manages to make lots of lovely swipes at the types who inhabit some of the creaky mentalities of contemporary Italy. There's the Equine butcher who has grown to understand that 'horsemeat was my vocation' and the Prefect of Carabinieri who, dismayed with endlessly rubber-stamping whatever the 'boys' have been up to progresses to taking on the 'invisible legions of evil', including the millions of malefactors who live inside water taps and take peeks at you when they think you're not looking.

The Voice of the Moon is a colourful satire, in the long and glorious tradition of Petronius Arbiter and Jonathan Swift. The director Federico Fellini, no mean satirist of contemporary Italy himself, has filmed *The Voice of the Moon*, to put beside his film masterwork based on Petronius' *Satyricon*. RL.

'This brought to my mind a gentleman from Pieve di Pino: "There was for example", I said, "a gentleman from Pieve di Pino who used to live surrounded by augers. They were spiral-shaped borers, and they were in the habit of extracting his thoughts, as well as pinching him, pulling his hair and weighing down on various parts of his body."' p158

CELATI
Gianni

Appearances [Quattro novelle sulle apparenze]

Like his other translated book *Voices From the Plains,* Celati's *Appearances* speaks of the flat North Italian plain and so is set far from the Tuscan idyll of cypresses and dark *Signorine* sighing in shuttered bedrooms of picture-book Italy. In fact things are grim at times but never humourless and the book is worth reading if only for the marvellous and sensually liberating *Conditions of Light on the Via Emilia*, the story of the landscape painter Emanuelle Menini, who 'knew very well how the light falls from the sky, how it touches and envelops things'. The story is a revelatory treatise on the quality of light and colours, illustrated both by vistas that are degraded — modern villa-homes with their 'overbright colours of the flowers in front of the doors and acrylic paints gleaming on the walls...the colours were all sharp like in a commercial traveller's book of samples' — and ones that are sublime, 'Finally as we went down the long road, he pointed out to us...the beautiful spring shadows in the ditches'.

The painter Menini, like the writer Celati, moves slowly through the world, looking at it with real attention and he is willing to share his appreciation, his hard-won knowledge of what the world really looks like, with us. RL

'On the phone he said: "Listen to me carefully, Luciano. Light and shade don't go well together these days because of the dirty air which doesn't give good shadows and then it gets into our lungs as well. And like drunks we try to make up for this by putting clear and lively colours everywhere, so that they can be seen better. But we get more and more drunk because the lively colours forget the shadows and the twilights and make you stupid — that's the fact of the matter.' p51

Voices from the Plain [Narratori delle Pianure]

A man chooses to spend some weeks travelling across the North Italian plain, going town by town through precisely the sort of landscape no-one ever *chooses* to travel in. A landscape where little cement villas clumped together impose their dreariness on the almost sarcastically flat plain of the River Po, a region that is industrialised and 'consumerised'. Celati, a kind of Italian George Orwell in his bleak and honest concern for the everyday, searches there for something profound. The stories in *Voices* are unornamented and unemphatic, influenced, perhaps, by the minimalist style that overtook American art and literature in the late 1970s; their apparent lack of emotion recalling the stories of Raymond Carver. Many of their characters — the young pharmacist who seduces the factory-owner's daughter, or the old printer who tries to write a pamphlet explaining 'what makes the world go on' — end up trapped in useless, obsessive acts. These very acts, Celati suggests, make up 'what life is: a web of ceremonial relationships which hold together something that has no substance.'

Celati has a particularly Italian sensitivity to landscape and in the story *A Japanese Girl* he transfers this sensitivity to Los Angeles, where to reach the house of the Japanese girl 'you had to leave the city freeway, cross enormous bridges packed with trucks and cars in all eight lanes, exit to the north and out into a canyon, keep going as far as the Arco station...' Here, landscape becomes the *absence* of landscape, of land-marks, of a sense of place. RL

'The Woman on the doorstep had not moved, but she no longer looked the man in the face as she had done. Now she was looking at the ground. Then, the one-eyed man headed towards the car parked in the threshing yard, and, on reaching the car, turned to speak to her. He told her that everything looks different when you feel yourself to be out in the open, when you stop believing you can hide somewhere and be safe.' pp122-123

COMENCINI
Cristina

The Missing Pages [Le Pagine Strappate]

Although only her first novel, Cristina Comenci arrives at the unwholesome heart of a central relationship — the one between father and daughter — with a firm narrative tread and the clearest of literary brush-strokes. Although it is lightly regarded in a culture where the maternal rules and all the emphasis is on the special bond with the male child, the awkwardness of the father/daughter encounter is here brought to light through the appearance of a psychosomatic condition in Frederica. She becomes completely silent with a case of aphasia or chronic speechlessness, a mysterious mechanism which is the unhappy result of a complex sequence of emotional events, to which only her diary is a witness. A very silent witness because the relevant pages have been torn out.

What happened in that irretrievable moment of memory, a moment forever inscribed into her consciousness and that robs her of the power to communicate? No-one understands her illness but somehow there is the mark of an accusation against the father, an accusation he is sure he can overcome as he overcomes everything in his life. But the invincibility which has won him a position in society and unchallenged authority over his family crumbles in the face of the misery of his daughter's condition. Federica's aphasia forces him into a dialogue with himself and deeply undermines him. He discovers then his own inability to speak, his own kind of silence, his emotional illiteracy.

The Missing Pages is the heartfelt, perhaps heartbroken work of a writer who puts her trust in the primacy of sentiment without being sentimental and in the power of words to speak the profundity of lived experience. FC

"'Federica, that's the way I am. I can reason, I can think, but that's it. I can't understand you and your problems, just as I've never been able to understand your sisters". He lowered his eyes. "Nor your mother properly, for that matter. Forgive me for spilling all these things out to you in this way, but I'm not used to talking about them."' p186

The Heart Of a Boy [Cuore]

Originally published in 1886, this is a patriotic hymn for the very young, written to celebrate (and instill) the values of a newly-united Italy. A teacher, welcoming the new Southern lad to his Northern classroom, sternly intones:

'Remember now what I am telling you. So that this could come about, that a Calabrian boy can be at home in Turin, and a boy from Turin can be at home in Reggio di Calabria, our country struggled for fifty years, and thirty thousand Italians died. You must all respect and love one another. If any of you should harm our companion because he was not born in our province, you would make yourself for ever more unworthy of raising your eyes from the ground when the tricolour goes by.'

DEL GIUDICE
Daniel

Lines of Light [Atlante Occidentale]

The ideal novel is Joseph Conrad's *Heart of Darkness* where a constant single theme — moral decay — is continually aligned with the image of a constant single thing; the river/the river-journey. The content of this great novel does not have to be hammered in by narrative or characterisation but instead seeps into consciousness through its unity of image, feeling and theme.

In *Lines of Light* instead of the river there is the Cyclotron, a huge circular tunnel under the Genevan countryside, itself the very image of rationality and in fact Voltaire's Castle stands (above ground) nearby. In this cool futuristic environment a scientist and a writer enter a dialogue. A dialogue reminiscent of good Science Fiction (Brian Aldiss, J.G.Ballard, Stanislaw Lem) because it touches on the *philosophical* rather than the emotional, moral or political realm. This is perhaps a very masculine book, celebrating, in a clean calm prose, the attempt to have dominion over the universe, by investigating, observing and shaping it. A dominion to be won through concentration and work, through involvement in a large project reaching into the future.

The dialogue of writer and scientist takes place substantially around flights in small planes, both men aspire 'to be above it all', both are exponents of an élite (and therefore spiritual?) consciousness. There is definitely a connection here to Herman Hesse's argument in his books *Steppenwolf* and *Journey to the East*. Like Hesse's best work *Lines of Light* is deeply refreshing and subtly mind-altering. RL

'Brahe gave a little nod. He thinks of their friendship, of that strange intimacy that comes from working together in isolation like this, through nights like this, in vast silent rooms like this, among huge machines, and insulated from the radiation by thick concrete blocks. They do not talk about their work except when absolutely necessary... In the tunnel that crossed the ring there were zones more roughhewn and zones where the floor and wall panels made interiors of blue-white light, with the background noise of the air conditioning, the coolers for the magnets, the fans. In the tunnel, the air was not air, and thoughts like "two in the morning" or "four in the afternoon" were totally irrelevant, time being represented only by sequences of numbers, numbers no different from those that indicated, on the screen, the birth and death of the lines.' p20

DELEDDA
Grazia

Cosima [Cosima]

Grazia Deledda was a noted writer of the 1920s from a poor corner of Sardinia and this is her only discernibly autobiographical work, where she tells the story of her childhood and youth, paying attention to interior realities as much as exterior ones. It's a diary in the form of a novel, written in the third person and with Cosima as the narrative double for the author herself. She is the 'serious dark-haired girl with large brown eyes and tiny hands and feet', very prone to daydream and reverie despite the 'restlessness of an Amazon', and 'passionate zeal of an adventure-story heroine' which is her basic nature.

The book is based on two themes; one the succession of events, the struggle with the world which matures the young girl's character — the death of her father and sister, the decline of her beloved brother Santus 'destined for great things' but destroyed by drink — while the other is the gradual development of her vocation as a writer. Here self-conquest develops from recognizing values beyond personal ambition and public success into an appreciation of individual strength: 'the whole self, drawing on the mystery of one's own inner life'.

> *Cosima* is an exceptionally interesting record of the development of a talented woman's artistic and human consciousness in a time and cultural climate which were not very easy for women in general. FC

'Now Cosima is again in her melancholy house where after her return from the mountain everything has taken on a sadder aspect, almost a decadence, or more precisely the withered damp colour of autumn — a funereal odour of chrysanthemums.

She is cold in the high road from whose window she sees Monte — it too already covered with fog. The crows' cry announces winter. But there are still moments for her when the sky opens wide and a springlike warmth heats her blood. She writes; bent over her scratch pad, when her sisters are looking after their mother, and Andrea is away in the country, and Santus is deep in one of his usual drunken sleeps, she throws herself into the world of her fantasies and writes, writes out of a physical need, like other adolescents run through garden paths or go to a forbidden place, and if they are able, to a rendezvous of love.' pp77-78

Elias Portolu [Elias Portolu]

Elias Portolu is an emblematic story of the head-on collision between the modern civilisation of bourgeois individualism and the archaic law of the clan which still prevails among the Sardinian people. The novel follows the story of a young man, Elias Portolu, returning to his native Sardinia from the mainland where he has spent several years in prison. His experience of prison life and the repressive methods of the new Italian state has left him uprooted. He is split between his nostalgia for a fixed value system he can become a part of — the island and its customs — and the longing to affirm his own independent personality. His discomfort develops into the tragedy of a guilt-ridden love that violates patriarchal law — that ancient and universal regulation which makes incest taboo — love of his sister-in-law. Incapable of firm resolve, (he is 'a youth as weak and beautiful as a woman'), he does not give full expression to his emotion, but nor can he manage to overcome it, overwhelmed as he is by a dark and persistent sense of guilt, alleviated only by his eventual decision to become a priest.

The motif of the book is the portrayal of the moral battle raging in Elias's conscience and, to a lesser degree, the battle which equally disturbs the soul of his sister-in-law Maddalena.

Torn between the temptation to yield to his emotions and the terror of the ensuing sin, between the desire for good and surrendering to evil, Elias chooses to abdicate from life and proclaim his own defeat. In this way he pays for his betrayal of his homeland through unhappiness.

Like a vast mirror, the harsh Sardinian landscape reflects the protagonist's fate, participating in the unfolding drama are the silences of the huge expanses of the *tancas* (fenced grazing lands), where nature accepts the sense of guilt which Elias keeps hidden from the community.

The novel has met with conflicting reviews in the years since its publication, but in this book Deledda progressed with assurance from her initial folklore-inspired work to psychological analysis, coming close to a completely mature style. FC

'The women prepared lunch, as usual, leaving the carving of the lamb to Zio Portolu; however, Maddalena obstinately followed Elias as though drawn by a magic thread, and every time he raised his eyes he met hers that seemed to want to bewitch him. Suddenly they were alone. Pietro had gone to the hunt, Mattia was chasing a lamb more restless than the others and Zio Portolu went to help him.

Elias had a moment of confusion, of fear, of indescribable pleasure at finding himself alone with Maddalena; alone amidst the grasses and high flowering thistle. His heart pounded and dizzy desire whirled through her being when his eyes met those passionate and pleading eyes of Maddalena.' p76

The Woman And The Priest [La Madre]

Structured like a classical tragedy, this is a 'Portrait in Black' of the harrowing conflict between love and duty, between an individual and the law. The conflict occurs within the narrow confines of a Sardinian village, but the themes it deals with are common — and fundamental — to all Mediterranean societies, and in particular to Italy.

There are three principle characters: a priest, a woman from the village with whom he falls in love, and his mother, who gives the book its original title. The illicit love affair is experienced with terrible remorse by the priest, who sees it conflicting with his role as the community's moral guide; his lover Agnese, on the other hand, fervently feels it to be her right. Between them stands the mother who, sitting atop the absolute hegemony furnished by Latin mentality and culture, drives her son to give up Agnese by using her powerful and demanding maternal love. She dies at the very moment of her triumph, returning the lovers to their individual existences beneath the burden of a shameful past.

From a sociological point of view, a particular virtue of this book is its portrayal of oppression: firstly by a religion which aims to dictate all values to each individual, and secondly by a mother's love, to which even men must defer. In this climate, woman becomes the diabolic and malevolent image of constant temptation, the sick and irredeemable creature that threatens collective stability. D.H. Lawrence writes in his preface to the English edition that Deledda 'creates the passionate complex of a primitive populace...the interest of the book lies, not in plot or characterisation, but in the presentation of sheer instinctive life.' FC

'She raised her face to his, her trembling lips, her lashes wet with tears. And his eyes were dazzled as by the glitter of deep waters, a glitter that blinds and beckons, and the face he gazed into was not the face of any woman on this earth — it was the face of Love itself. And he fell forward into her arms and kissed her upon the mouth.' p187

DURANTI
Francesca
Happy Ending [Lieto Fine]

And it really does have a happy ending — beautiful, romantic, even realistic. Duranti takes a very classical format; a family, a fading head of the family, an interloper who rocks the boat of everyday life and a series of adults who refuse to grow up — and she elegantly arranges the pieces to form a tale of continuity and renewal. The book is a very beguiling expression of the Italian ideal of family as an association of mutual concern, a source of all-accepting, spoiling love — a vision that will perhaps seem even more ideal to readers in the Anglo-Saxon world, where impersonal societies don't seem to encourage much more than a small unit of consumption, a generator of shopping lists.

Ideal or not, the issues that arise within a family are not skipped here: *authority* for example, personified by the family's female head who doesn't allow herself a moment's rest from being in control ('Authority is a way of walking, of speaking to the dog, of opening a door'). A well-crafted story. RL

"'Get hold of time and gather all its moments together so that they won't disperse like a flock without a shepherd. Each instant should mark at once the accomplishment of an old commitment and the promise of a new one. Never live 'at random', never say 'I can't'. Above all, and most crucially, never look for an excuse: to reign simply means there is no one to call in sick to.'" p149

The House On Moon Lake [La Casa Sul Lago Della Luna]

This is the story of a rare specimen: a male with a complicated, neurotic, 'feminine' character, who is both attracted to and repulsed by his strong and sensible modern girlfriend. There's a good amount of role reversal in the feminine but sexually flexible image of possession proffered here: *she* is the one who 'possessed him and penetrated him...and she was the one who decided when to leave without saying a word.'

Duranti's titillating but intelligent look at the femininized condition the male protagonist Fabrizio, a literary translator by profession, slips into and which extends to quasi-occult regions as Fabrizio, at work, feels himself being 'permeated and possessed by the Other' — merging with the author he is translating. Perhaps though Duranti is depicting something less than occult: the process a translator lives through when engaged in a long and intensely close relationship with his or her subject. A translator has to understand an author's every nuance, every heightening, twist or weighting of words and render them into his own language can be carried right up to the boundaries of his personality and to those of another. The theme might produce in a reader far wider reflections than just those that preoccupy translators.

Another major theme of the book, perhaps a very Northern Italian or Middle European one (Northern Italy is also part of Mitteleuropa) is that of *inheritance*. One could understand from a few lines of *The House On Moon Lake* more than one could from all those fat family sagas that torment the shelves of W.H.Smith what a *lineage* might be, what ideals could be extracted from it and how it could be something to preserve or to create or imagine if found to be absent. RL

'Fulvia was made of different stuff. Her moral toughness, her loyalty, her sincerity, her faithfulness to bargains, were absolute: there was never any question that she could look after herself and knew what was coming to her. That was her style, the mark of the great, old, noble stock of Adelmo Basso, the cooper; it was something that could not be bought or taught — a system, a universe of objects, laws and memories so ingrained that it entered the blood and became second nature: a legacy, the only possession one could avail oneself of with genuine confidence...a cornerstone on which to build subsequent constructions, a solid base to rest on or to take off from, a standard for relations with others and a model for solitude...' p80

FALLACI
Oriana

Letter to a Child Never Born [Lettere a un Bambino Mai Nato]

The book that made Fallaci famous is a piece of writing that lies somewhere between fiction and confession. It's a long letter written by a woman to the baby she is carrying in her womb, beginning at the moment when she learns of its existence and ending when this existence ceases. The monologue, addressed to an audience that has no opportunity to respond, confronts the complexities bound up in the choice of motherhood and the struggle of a woman who resolves to have a baby on her own.

The conflict with the man who opposes her decision, the argument with the girlfriend who urges her to think of her career, the difficult relationship with the doctors who don't consider her, a single woman, to be a 'proper' mother, are initially obstacles which she is proud to stand up to. But when the pregnancy begins to demand a radical change of life from her, a total renunciation of her participation in the world, these voices torment her in her solitude. Her determination slowly gives way to uncertainty, triggering in her a process of rebellion against her condition, against another life which threatens her own. She loses the child and accepts its disappearance just as she accepted the proclamation of life: 'You're dead but I am alive. So alive that I don't regret it, and I don't accept trials, I don't accept verdicts, not even your forgiveness.'

Avoiding facile rhetoric, the book pursues a clear objective: to open up discussion on the question of women's free will in motherhood, to acknowledge a woman's exclusive, cognizant rule over her own life. FC

'Yes, it was while I was shouting like this that I heard your voice: "Mother!" And I felt a sense of loss — of emptiness — because it was the first time anyone had called me Mother, and because it was the first time I was hearing your voice, and it wasn't the voice of a child. And I thought: "He was a man!" Then I thought: "He was a man, he'll condemn me". Finally I thought: "I want to see him!" And my eyes searched everywhere, in the cage, outside the cage, among the benches, beyond the benches, on the floor, on the walls. But they didn't find you. You weren't there. There was only the quiet of a tomb. And in this quiet of a tomb your voice was heard again: "Mother! Let me speak, Mother. Don't be afraid. There's no need to be afraid of the truth."' p86

FLAIANO
Ennio

A Time to Kill [Tempo di Uccidere]

Just after the second world war, while other Italian novelists were focusing 'neo-realistically' on recent events, Flaiano decided to cast his gaze further back to another war. This was the Abyssinian War of 1936 in which the Fascist Regime planned to assert Italy's destiny as a colonial power. Flaiano produces a picture that is very far from the high-sounding rhetoric of conquest. The book's protagonist accidentally wounds an innocent native woman in the forest — the same woman who gave herself unfeigningly to him in a night of love — and he has to kill her, thereby soiling himself with an act of the most shameful violence. From here on he falls into an appalling spiral of evil, a terrible chain of events afflict him, beginning with an illness that he has perhaps picked up in that fleeting relationship and that seems like the woman's implacable vendetta against him. Africa becomes a realm of contagion for this anti-hero who is the incarnation of the ordinary man caught up in a pitiless adventure which, at heart, he has no conscience for.

The book won the first Strega Prize in 1947 and Flaiano went on to collaborate on the films of Fellini and Pasolini. FC

'It was not a good film and yet I had seen it several times. Every day, although I was beginning to be ashamed of this weakness, I left, I left the hotel determined to have a stroll; I went as far as the gardens, looked at the valley, went into a bar to drink an apéritif and then, insensibly, there I was in front of the stills of that film I had already seen so often, in Italy too. I was afraid the cashier would recognise me that day and be amazed at such stubborn constancy, but she did not recognise me and a little later I was deep in the muffled narcotic calm of the dream.

I knew why the film made me so calm. There was something in the eyes of a supporting actress — oh, nothing special! — something which reminded me of other eyes. An overpowering peace comforted me when those eyes rolled on the screen; I gave myself up to them and tried to live with her memory, to retrace in my most forgotten memories the moments of our happiness. And I was ashamed of it.' pp68-69

GADDA
Carlo Emilio

That Awful Mess on the Via Merulana [Quer Pasticcio Brutto de Via Merulana]

Written in a polyphony of voices and dialects, Gadda's detective stories are unique in Italian literature. This story is a real 'mess', dominated by the figure of an investigator, Doctor Francesco Ingravallo, who has had to resignedly accept a transfer to the capital. He is given the job of sorting out the intricate crime committed in the Via Merulana, in a condominium housing an avaricious population of shopkeepers, businessmen, well-off professionals and profiteers.

Against the background of a Rome where fascism is preparing its final take-over — the year is 1927 and Mussolini is making the transition from Prime Minister to Fascist 'Duce' ('Führer') — a woman Ingravallo knows, Liliana, is murdered, and, a few days later, a neighbouring woman is attacked and robbed. These events run into one another, become more complicated, one obscures the other and gradually new characters are brought on who seem to be essential to the resolution of the crime but actually only muddle things further.

The worried Ingravallo tries to 'twitch the strings of the inert puppet of probability' and ends up feeling the ground beneath his feet slip away, sure of having got to the bottom of the affair and, finding himself face-to-face with the guilty party, guilt is denied for the umpteenth time.

With amazing effect Gadda then delivers the conclusion to the story, pointing out that what is vital is not the discovery of the guilty party but everything around the crime, the chain of causation that allowed evil to act yet again. FC

'From the right, where the plain was dense with dwellings and went down to the river, Rome appeared, lying as if on a map or a scale model: it smoked slightly, at Porta San Paolo: a clear proximity of infinite thoughts and palaces, where the north wind had cleansed, which the tepid succession of sirocco had after a few hours, with its habitual knavishness, resolved in easy images and had gently washed. The cupola of mother-of-pearl: other domes, towers: dark clumps of pines. Here ashen: there all pink and white, confirmation veils: sugar in a *haute pâté,* a morning painting by Sciajola. It looked like a huge clock flattened on to the ground, which the chain of the Claudian aqueduct bound....joined....to the mysterious springs of the dream. There, stood the general HQ of the forces: there, there, for many moons, his dreamed-of application lay waiting, waiting. Like pears, medlars, even an application's ripening is marked by that capacity for perfectable maceration which the capital of the ex-kingdom confers on all paper, is commensurate with an unrevolving time, but internal to the paper and its relative stamps, a period of incubation and of Roman softening. Bedecked, with silent dust, are all of the red tapes, the dossiers of the files: with heavy cobwebs, all the great boxes of time: of the incubating time, *Roma doma*; Rome tames, Rome broods. On the hay-stack of her decrees. A day comes, at last when the egg of the longed-for promulgation drops at last from her viscera, from the sewer of the decretal labyrinth: and the respective rescript, which licenses the gaunt petitioner to scramble that egg for the rest of his natural life, is whipped off to the addressee. In more cases than one, it arrives along with Extreme Unction. It licenses the applicant, now sunk into coma — *verba volant, scripta manent* — to practise that sleeping art, that crippled trade that he had surreptitiously practised until then, till the moment of the Holy Oil: and which from then on, *de jure decreto*, he will make an effort to practise, a little at a time, in hell with all the leisure granted him by eternity.' pp264-5

GINZBURG
Natalia

The Manzoni Family [La Famiglia Manzoni]

Natalia Ginzburg herself said of this work about the family of Alessandro Manzoni, author of the great Italian classic *The Betrothed*;

'I have tried to piece together the history of the Manzoni family; I wanted to rebuild it, recompose it, arrange it systematically in time. I have some letters and some books. I didn't want to give (my own) comments, but to keep myself to a simple, naked order of events. I wanted events to speak for themselves. I wanted the letters, sad or cold, ceremonious or straight-forward, obviously untruthful or un-

doubtedly sincere, to speak for themselves. And yet it gradually became clear to me that it was impossible not to make some comments. They are, however, rare and brief. I didn't want the central figure of this long family history to be Alessandro Manzoni. A family history doesn't have one single protagonist; each one of its members is in the spotlight and then pushed back into the shadows, at various times. I didn't want him to have more space than the others; I want him to be glimpsed, seen in profile and mixed in with the others, enveloped in the dust clouds of daily life. And yet he dominates the scene, he is the head of the family; and the others undoubtedly don't have his stature. And also he appears, more than the others, to be strange, tortuous and complex. In some rare instances it was impossible for me not to observe him full in the face and standing apart.'

Voices In The Evening [Le Voci della Sera]

Voices covers Ginzburg's favourite terrain, family life, awkwardly realistic family life and she is working at the height of her style which is a powerful and seducing *matter-of-factness*. How matter-of-factness can be so seductive, so surprising and real is her great skill, her great achievement as a writer.

Ginzburg, whose husband died under Nazi torture, seems to feel the beauty of the everyday particularly sharply and alongside the kind humour of her half-bitchy, half-affectionate family conversations there is a melancholy realism. RL

'"Because after she had lost her voice," said my mother, "she went practically mad through grief and was treated in a clinic. Once a week a dentist visited the place to see the patients' teeth, and thus he fell in love with her. She had a very beautiful mouth."

"You have told this story to me millions of times," said my father. "Why do you want to bother Tommasino with it, with persons he has never seen and never will see?"

"It serves to make a bit of conversation," said my mother. Do you want us to sit here all evening gazing into each other's eyes? One tells stories and talks, someone says one thing, and someone else another."'
p136

The Little Virtues [Le Piccole Virtù]

This is an extraordinary book, a pure act of generosity by its author, who has managed to share her wry, humane and spirited take on life with the reader. From this collection of eleven short pieces, particularly of note are *My Vocation*, in which Ginzburg speaks of her life as a writer in terms that will cheer anyone who has genuinely dedicated themselves to a profession or art; the two hilarious, charming sketches of England, *England: Eulogy and Lament* and *La Maison Volpé* ; and *Portrait of a Friend*, her panegyric to Cesare Pavese. Although outside the mainstream of her work, which is the novella of family affairs, *The Little Virtues* is perhaps Ginzburg's greatest (and most contemporary) achievement. RL

'Our friend lived in the city as an adolescent, and he lived in the same way until the end. His days were extremely long and full of time, like an adolescent's; he knew how to find time to study and to write, to earn his living and to wander idly through the streets he loved; whereas we, who staggered from laziness to frantic activity and back again, wasted our time trying to decide whether we were lazy or industrious...at times he was very unhappy, but for a long time we thought that he would be cured of this unhappiness when he decided to become an adult; his unhappiness seemed like that of a boy — the absent-minded voluptuous melancholy of a boy who has not yet got his feet on the ground and who lives in the sterile, solitary world of his dreams.' p15

GIOVENE
Andrea

The Book Of Sansevero [L'Autobiografia di Giuliano di Sansevero]

An enormous book, the fictionalised autobiography of Giuliano Sansevero, scion of a noble Neapolitan family fallen on hard times through the worthlessness of its latter generations. Giuliano is called upon to restore the family fortunes and here is the story of his life; childhood in a Gormenghast-like castle, his education in an austere monastery, followed by his acceptance and then rejection of the burden his family has laid on him.

Like Mervyn Peake's *Gormenghast* trilogy, the book is rich in characters and atmospheres; but unlike *Gormenghast Sansevero* is quite unambiguously set in the modern world, beginning in 1912. Political events such as the labour strikes and demonstrations after the end of World War One and the Fascist takeover of 1922 show up, diffracted through the lenses of various members of Giuliano's large, often bizarre family. This view from society's upper echelons is carried out with a consistency that makes the book an authentic portrait of its times; its panorama of mid-century Europe takes Giuliano to Milan, Paris, Ischia, then as an officer to Occupied Greece and finally to the Götterdämmerung before Berlin as the Red Army sweeps in to crush Hitler's last stand.

A fascinating book, full of accurate history and psychological insight into the mind of a diffident but cultivated man. RL

'one entered a second room, also very dark, and inhabited by a decrepit parrot as motionless as a stuffed bird on its perch, but which, on hearing a sound, roused itself and shrieked its own name, which was the usual one of Polly...on a long verandah with hexagonal panes, whitish alternating with Prussian blue, four aged people sat immobile in a row at approximately equal distances from each other, in enormous armchairs like statues in a museum...And the great-aunts and uncles, the one blind, the other paralysed, the third obese, sat there without moving, and this for days, months, years, in a solemn and fearful silence broken only, from time to time, by Polly's raucous cry.' p31

Sweet Days of Discipline [I Beati Anni del Castigo]

This is the evocation of a self-absorbed childhood in an atmosphere bleached by memory and the passage of the years. The narrator awaits her release from a dull boarding school in which everything seems to have been programmed and pre-ordained.

It is also that irrepeatable time of life filled with first discoveries, every step taken a step nearer to what is real because in the school existence is totally subordinated to a system, a system where everything has been pre-arranged — as if it had in fact already happened. The only thing left to chance is a love to share this imprisonment with, and this book tells its story. The narrator's love for Fréderique is the only 'deviation', the only individual act in a place that doesn't provide for any freedom or rather has taken account of this too as yet another constraint, another inevitable fact.

With a distant echo of Robert Musil's *The Confessions of Young Törless* the book engages the development of a rather different kind of adolescence, different from the usual differences because this is an aristocratic adolescence but no less significant for that and it is one that forever reverberates through one's consciousness. FC

'One winter afternoon — we were sitting on the stairs — Frédérique took my hands and said: "You've got an old woman's hands." Hers were cold. She turned them over: they were shrivelled up. I can hardly describe how proud I was to hear what for me was a compliment. That day, on the stairs, I knew she was attracted to me. They really were an old woman's hands, they were bony. Frédérique's hands were broad, thick, square, like a boy's. Both of us wore signet rings on our little fingers. You might imagine that we found physical pleasure in touching each other like this. As she touched my hand and I felt hers, cold, our contact was so anatomical that the thought of flesh or sensuality eluded us.' p18

LAMPEDUSA
Giuseppe Tommasi di
The Leopard [Il Gattopardo]

In the Salina coat of arms, the long-whiskered leopard is the symbol of an ancient power whose last glorious representative is Prince Fabrizio. Colossal and eccentric, he looms over the entire novel, which paints a picture of the Sicilian aristocracy when, after the arrival of Garibaldi's forces in 1860, a new class, the bourgeoisie, were coming to power. A counterpoint to the figure of the prince is his young nephew Tancredi, a new man who paves the way for the ascent of this enterprising middle class. His liberal ideas and marriage to Angelica Sedara, daughter of a shrewd and prosperous peasant, mark the gradual loss of power that is the historical fate of the Salina lineage. The price watches his ancient household and its august strength being 'corrupted' and is left the only survivor of an eclipsed world, a spectator, a passive leopard whose claws no longer have the power of life or death.

Written in 1956 but only discovered after its author's death in 1958, the novel became a *cause célèbre* and enjoyed immediate success as the product of a great narrator. Since then it has become a literary classic, translated into many languages, made famous in an unforgettable film by Lucchino Visconti in the 1960s. FC

'His arrival was greeted with happy tears. He embraced and blessed his mother, whose deep widow's weeds set off nicely her white hair and rosy hue... As soon as he got into the house he was assailed as always by sweet youthful memories. Nothing was changed, from the red brick floor to the sparse furniture; the same light entered the small narrow windows; Romeo, the dog, barking briefly in a corner, was exactly like another hound, its great-great-grandfather, his companion in violent play; and from the kitchen arose the centuries-old aroma of simmering stew of essence of tomatoes, onions and mutton, for macaroni on festive occasions.' pp155-6

An Autumn Story [Racconto d'autunno]

Landolfi's only novel to appear in English will please those who like Gothic: though written by a contemporary writer (he died in 1975) and set in the mid-twentieth century, the novel seems a throwback to that nineteenth-century genre. This is a book about strange passions, obsession, solitude, concealment and confinement. It makes its way through dark Jungian abysses... RL

'their passion, rather than calming down or becoming more tolerable, blazed so intensely that it took on bizarre, excessive, even fearfully violent forms and manifestations...The husband's adoration was so overwhelming that he actually set up an altar, on which the young woman had to remain, nude, for several hours of the day and especially the night, in front of burning candles and amid clouds of incense.' p121

Christ Stopped at Eboli [Cristo e Fermato a Eboli]

Christ Stopped at Eboli is perhaps one of the great books of our century. Its effective, convincing humanism seeks to breed understanding and widen mental horizons. Half-anthropology and half-literature, it's also a book that any travel writer would give up their life to have written.

As a young Turin intellectual with the courage publicly to oppose Mussolini, Levi was sent into juridical exile in a tiny village in Italy's deep South. There, far from the centres of power and culture, he discovered a peasant world that was impoverished, exhausted and marginalised but with its own ancient roots in the local landscape and culture. In describing it he achieves a tender warmth of tone and imagery that would produce a sympathy for other kinds of lives in any reader.

Beyond being a book about a backward and forgotten region of Italy, this is an unsurpassed essay on what Levi calls 'history outside the framework of time'. It shows how when we eat a husk of bread dipped in olive oil and salt we touch a Mediterranean experience that has existed for at least three thousand years and taste the same taste as Homer and know we stand under the same sun as he did. Similarly, in his evocative description of the landscape and the everyday life of its people Levi tried to break through the barriers of education and prejudice that separated him from these people and immerse himself and the reader in a human world that transcends its time and place. RL

'Death was in the house: I loved these peasants and I was sad and humiliated by my powerlessness against it. Why, then, at the same time, did a great feeling of peace pervade me? I felt detached from every earthly thing and place, lost in a no man's land far from time and reality. I was hidden, like a shoot under the bark of a tree, beyond the reach of man. I listened to the silence of the night and felt as if I had all of a sudden penetrated the very heart of the universe. An immense happiness, such as I had never known, swept over me with a flow of fulfillment.' p214

LEVI
Primo

The Drowned and the Saved [I Sommersi e i Salvati]

In this internationally celebrated book, Primo Levi, a Jewish-Italian concentration camp survivor, leaves a harrowing testament. Most importantly he accuses the German people of the collective crime of cowardice — cowardice in looking away from the system of human extermination set up in their name. He calls the whole existence of Nazi Germany 'a war against memory' and, for this reason perhaps, was moved to make the sacrifice of reliving his own memories of that period, an act that might have contributed to his sudden death shortly after the book's completion. From the chapter *The Grey Zone* one realises that the 'work' of the camps was huge, consistent and well-organised, and went on for years; it could not have been merely the enterprise of a few SS zealots.

Levi highlights something infinitely depressing: the opportunism of German officers, functionaries and business-men who simply didn't want to pass up the opportunities for promotion and profit that the concentration camp system offered them; many of these people later hid behind the excuse of being forced to obey, although they might well have sidestepped orders. Moreover, writes Levi, the ghastly glimmer of the 'drowned world' illuminates a wider one, the mechanisms of irresponsible power being equivalent: the political criminals of today, for example, stand firmly in the footsteps of the Nazi pioneers of civilised barbarity. And Hitler in any case *did* permanently change the world: this is the hardest fact to face for all the European survivors of fascism and World War Two, Jews and Gentiles alike. Two generations have grown up in a racially 'purified' Europe and must face and act upon 'the shame that the Germans never knew, the shame which the just man experiences when confronted by a crime committed by another.'

This is an important book not only because it documents the *Shoah* or holocaust but also because so many fundamental questions are raised by the reflections of a man who was a witness and struggled to survive and, yet more heroically, to understand these events.

Levi tried to remember fragments of Dante in the death camp because 'they made it possible for me to re-establish a link with the past, saving it from oblivion and reinforcing my identity'. This search for cultural and psychological continuity in terrible conditions contrasts with the Europe that in 1945 sought to forget its recent past, immersing itself in dreams of building a socialist utopia in the East and a capitalist, consumer one in the West: two Brave New Worlds suffering from the same amnesia, a disregard for an inheritance in equal proportion magnificent and ugly, half-Mozart, half-Hitler. If today's re-united continent is to retrace its steps, rediscover itself, accept and learn from its whole history, then the path leads through Belsen and Levi has written a guide. RL

'So I realised that the German of the Lager — skeletal, howled, studded with obscenities and imprecations — was only vaguely related to the precise, austere language of my chemistry books, and to the melodious, re-fined German of Heine's poetry that Clara, a classmate of mine, would recite to me.' pp75-76

If This is a Man & The Truce [Se Questo e un Uomo & La Tregua]

Primo Levi was a young, educated and inept member of the Italian resistance when he was captured by the fascist militia in the winter of 1943. He was identified as a Jew and shipped to Auschwitz. This book is an account of his time in hell until the liberation, and (in its second part) how he managed to make his way home in the chaos of post-war Europe.

It has already attracted so many superlatives — 'one of the century's truly necessary books', writes Paul Bailey — that the chief danger is that people will ignore it for that very reason, as they tend to do things which too many people say would be good for them. That would be a great pity, since it is not only a record of the ultimate expression of Nazism it is also a profound testament of and to all humanity. And it is beautifully written — as elegant, economical, and dispassionate as its subject-matter is horrific and emotionally overwhelming. The effect of this conjunction is uniquely poignant.

The immense camp where Levi and his fellow-prisoners suffered and mostly died never produced a pound of synthetic rubber, which was its ostensible purpose. Its real purpose was death. On one occasion, denied even an icicle to assuage thirst, he asked in his broken German, '*Warum?*' The guard replied, '*Hier ist kein warum*' (there is no why here).

Everything about such a life was a deliberate denial of human dignity. Survival itself was largely a matter of chance, mitigated, for a few, only by falling on the right side of the ferocious law, 'to he that has, will be given; from he that has not, will be taken away'. Levi's dignity is therefore all the more authentic and moving for having been so dearly bought. No mere luxury, it was what he survived for, and what he has given to us.

The years since Levi's death have increasingly confirmed what he and his fellow ex-prisoners felt in post-liberation Vienna: 'not compassion, but a larger anguish, which was mixed up with our own misery, with the heavy, threatening sensation of an irreparable and definitive evil which was present everywhere, nestling like gangrene in the guts of Europe and the world, the seed of future harm.' No one should think that what has happened could not happen again; and for anyone who finds that an appalling prospect, this book is (as Levi puts it in his Afterword) 'a support and a warning'. It is also, by the same token, a reminder that literature itself is not an ornament of civilization but integral to it. PC

'Monsters exist, but they are too few in number to be truly dangerous. More dangerous are the common men, the functionaries ready to believe and to act without asking questions...' p396

Moments of Reprieve [Lilit e Altri Racconti]

Like the *Drowned and the Saved* and *If This is a Man* this is one of the series of books Primo Levi wrote about his and others' experience of the German death camps. Levi strove, as all men and women with any social awareness must, to draw lessons for the future from this descent into scientific cruelty and morbid nihilism. In this particular book he chose to pick out stories he had witnessed or that were recounted to him of individuals who escaped, for a moment or for a lifetime, the grisly extermination machine of the Nazis. Levi himself called these escapes 'breaches...in the black universe' and it is the unprecedented background of the camps that makes the lives and events he describes so shining.

There is the glitter of the Lillith story told amongst desperate men (*Lillith*), a vision of the Hitler Youth being shown around the camp in late 1944 to see 'the enemy, the submen who were destroying Germany' (*Last Christmas of the War*) and the poignant story of Rappoport with his strange balance sheet of pleasure and pain (*Rappoport's Testament*). *Moments of Reprieve* joins those other books by Jewish writers like Bassani and S.Y.Agnon touched by the Holocaust as a statement about the unspeakable and the unthinkable. That horrified silence is, today, a part of the barrier the Nazis built around their deeds, like the wire fences of their camps, a barrier that still needs to be torn down — which makes these writers' elliptical method of suggesting something by never quite mentioning it an effective and humane way to proceed. RL

'It often happens these days that you hear people say they're ashamed of being Italian. In fact we have good reasons too be ashamed: first and foremost, of not having been able to produce a political class that represents us and, on the contrary, tolerating for thirty years one that does not. On the other hand, we have virtues of which we are unaware, and we do not realize how rare they are in Europe and in the world.' p117

The Wrench [Le Chiave a Stella]

Primo Levi worked for many years as an industrial chemist before becoming a full-time writer and *The Wrench* is his tribute to the skills and lifestyle of those who work with hand and brain. We meet Faussone, a rigger who builds derricks and cranes and who has knocked around the world a fair bit on various jobs. Faussone embodies the dignity and beauty of labour and skill. The privilege of loving one's work, 'the most concrete approximation of happiness on earth', is enjoyed by Faussone and his old father, who in his time made copper pans by hand and passed on to his son the craftsman's tradition of taking pride in one's own creation. RL

'This was the central subject, and I realized Faussone knew it. If we except those miraculous and isolated moments fate can bestow on a man, loving your work (unfortunately, the privilege of a few) represents the best, most concrete approximation of happiness on earth. But this is a truth not many know. This boundless region, the region of *le boulot*, the job, *il rusco* – of daily work, in other words – is less known than the Antarctic, and through a sad and mysterious phenomenon it happens that people who talk most, and loudest, about it are the very ones who have never travelled through it..' p80 *Beating Copper*

LOY
Rosetta

The Dust Roads of Montferrato [Le Strade di Polvere]

This book follows the lives of three generations of extraordinary characters who occupy a farm in Piedmont, Northern Italy, from the late eighteenth century, when Napoleon's armies come marching through, to the days when the first factories start to appear outside the local city walls. Its overview of history is interesting in itself, particularly as it reveals that France, rather than Italy (a nation not yet created), was the *metropole*, the source of ideas, fashions and even songs for these North-Easterners.

One great strength of Loy's book is that it makes space, as does Marquez's *One Hundred Years Of Solitude*, for the 'peculiarness' of life, for bizarre characters who crop up in family lines. Another is that it undertakes a fertile exposition of what one might call the 'woman's' (rather than the 'feminist') ideology in its representation of women protagonists as the strong, real people, of the beauty of children and of the domestic space as the real theatre of life. Battles, *coups d'état*, politics, even agricultural work all take place off-stage here, important only insofar as they affect women as mothers, wives, matrons and matriarchs. Men, moreover, are generally seen as gorgeous, delicate creatures, stallions with brittle legs and sensitive ears, objects of female desire, hopefully but not often turning into good providers and stewards in later life. Perhaps a woman younger than Loy (presently in her early fifties) couldn't have written like this, and would have brought to her writing a degree of scepticism about traditional family arrangements...

Be that as it may, Loy's descriptions of her female characters is truly a wonder, perhaps owing something to the Italian cultural fixation with beauty — from which comes the notion that external appearance reflects the soul, very different from the Protestant, Northern idea, which expects to find inner purity under an exterior plainness. The Italian vision, the Italian celebration of beauty is perhaps the same one that helped make Italians such great painters during the Renaissance. RL

'Luis' first wife was the Maturlins' Teresina. She was, as everyone would have expected, plump just where plumpness was necessary and she had fiery hair. Not tawny like the smith's daughter but a barley blonde, intense and thick...The Maturlins' Teresina played the spinet and she used her table-napkin with such grace that it was a pleasure to watch her eat...Her great passion was the *rusnent*, the rust apples, which she gathered by herself and ate at all hours, biting deep into them with her strong, little teeth, neatly aligned. She also loved the blossoms of those apples and during the spring she spent in the house she would put them in her hair and at dusk, wilted, they would fall to the ground, a sign of her luminous passage.' pp108-9

MAGRIS
Claudio

Danube [Danubio]

Danube is not exactly a work of fiction but the story of a great river and of a major civilisation. It's also, more modestly, a book that speculates about how it might be possible to tell such a story, one that has to travel through so much geography (from the Black Forest to the Black Sea) and so much history (from just before the Romans to just before the fall of the Berlin Wall).

It's a fabulous journey made by a scholar and writer who is himself fabulously erudite on the German-led culture of Central Europe. This is a journey through space and time with a guide rather different from our familiar Anglo-Saxon travel writers who proudly parade their ignorance and are therefore always *discovering* things. Magris in contrast is always *finding* things he already knows a great deal about, and can shed the light of his learning onto them. This is not a package tour of Central and South-Eastern Europe but a journey full of meetings with the remarkable men of a whole millennium.

Magris makes his journey in the company of a great list of famous and lesser-known artists and scholars who have some connection with places along the great river basin. He picks up the scent of Louis-Fernand Céline, the *genie maudite* of modern French literature, author of *Journey to the End of the Night,* in the Castle of Sigmaringen where, in the last days of World War II he stayed with Marshal Pétain's collaborationist French government-in-exile, awaiting the Götterdämmerung of total defeat. Magris also wanders down many minor, and charming, by-ways of German and Austrian literature where it is doubtful if many readers will follow him — accepting that a Professor of German Literature like Magris has a rather special idea of what constitutes interesting reading. On the other hand, further down river in Austria we hear about Franz Kafka's last weekend on earth.

This is a history in footnotes, a delightful thing, full of extraordinary news of Captains and Kings, of great and lesser writers but also of Jewish umbrella-makers and a plump schoolmaster who showed the young Magris the meaning of right and wrong. In there too is something about the Shamanistic religion of the Early Hungarians and the strange story of the German cities of the East...

Reading all this one ends with the feeling that more than having read a book one has made an investment, and acquired the sense of an almost suffocatingly rich history and culture; a Viennese pastry laden with cream and liqueur, an elaborate street façade in Old Budapest, a week in Balkan politics.

Mitteleuropa was once another great melting-pot and from one of its corners (Claudio Magris' home city of Trieste, formerly the port city of Austro-Hungary) it has found a worthy spokesman and interpreter. This is a wonderful introduction to its riches. RL

'German culture, side by side with Jewish culture, has been the unifying factor and germ of civilization in central Eastern Europe. The town squares of Sibiu-Hermannstadt and Brasov-Kronstadt, images of a German tradition that may well no longer exist in Germany itself, are like the ancient Roman arches and aqueducts: the seal and stamp of an integrated culture which bestowed a face on Central Europe.' p309

A Different Sea [Un Altro Mare]

Magris' novella is a masterpiece that manages both to be philosophical and to rescue a part of Italian history: the period during which Gorizia, near Trieste, was the 'Hapsburg Nice'. The book's protagonist Enrico, brought up in the multicultural embrace of the late Austro-Hungarian Empire (which held lands inhabited by Italian, Slav and German-speakers in the area where Ex-Yugoslavia and Italy meet), sails off to Patagonia to carve out for himself a simple and honourable existence. This book covers the distance between Europe and South America, between adolescence and middle age, between classical and contemporary values. Its story of voluntary renunciation of material well-being and human company is so out of keeping with the inflamed consumerism of today that it can exert a real force on the reader.

Written with economy and power, *A Different Sea* is perhaps one of the best works of contemporary Italian literature. Magris, who can be prodigious as a writer (his *Danube* runs for 416 pages) has here produced a sparkling little book for seekers after truth, as good an account of a man's spiritual trajectory as Herman Hesse's marvellous *Journey To The East*. RL

'Nussbaumer was right to insist that Greek be translated into German, for they are the two indispensable languages, perhaps the only languages in which birth and death can be discussed. Italian is different. Italian for him is not the language of statements, or of definitions which stun with their brightness or their space. Instead it is the language of postponement, of digression, the language for coming to terms with the unbearable, for keeping destiny at bay for a while by dint of constant chatter. In short, Italian is the language of life, the language of reconciliation, of indebtedness like life itself, or, at most, like a suit — worn to satisfy social convention.' p9

Inferences On A Sabre [Illazioni Su una Sciabola]

This is a true story although its main protagonist was a romantic novelist. He was Krasnov, an exiled (and retired) Russian general who starred in a piece of murderous play-acting sponsored by Nazi Germany in its last year of power. Under its auspices he led a group of exiles (Cossacks and other refugees from Bolshevik Russia) into victimising the a region of North-Eastern Italy. Magris illuminates a forgotten corner of World War Two, telling his story in a way that preserves all the ambiguities of real life, suggesting that history books are the real fiction, with their neat categories and judgements...

Above all it is a story of tangled motives. The displaced Cossacks were themselves historical victims creating more victims under their elderly novelist-general, a natural leader and perhaps naturally honourable man who served a dishonourable cause.

As an 'Austro-Hungarian' Italian Magris is sympathetic to the displaced, the people who must wander, the forsaken creatures of dead empires. This short set piece of a book is an excellent example of how to look at conflicts and wars for the tangled webs of history that lie behind them. RL

'That broken sabre, that bladeless hilt surfacing from the broken grave, brings to mind a sight I haven't seen for years now, not since my legs became too weak to take me up into the woods on Monte Nevoso, where the old eastern border of Italy once ran, and where the boundary now lies between Slovenia and Croatia. If you climb up through the trees toward a hollow called Tri Kalici, beneath the summit, at a certain point you will reach — or used to reach, but it's sure to be there still — the trunk of a felled tree; the tree had been dead a long time and was already withered and decayed into the ground, though not completely. I climbed up to Tri Kalici many times, year after year, and that tree was always there, every year more decomposed and close to dissolving into the earth, but still itself, with its own form, or the memory of its form. As I passed by, I would greet it like a brother and, watching it unmake itself while preserving its individuality, I could accept its fate — feeling it was my fate too, which every passing year brings closer — without fear, almost reverently, affectionately.' p83

The Skin [La Pelle]

This novel gives a truthful account of the spiritual condition of a liberated but defeated Europe, documenting the mood of nihilism, the moral dissolution and the existential nausea of a conquered people. History intertwines with narrative against the backdrop of Naples, a city in despair, gripped by the plague which coincided with the arrival of the Allied forces in October 1943. The city is portrayed as a place of degradation and degeneracy, condemned to a corruption that touches and contaminates everything. The powerless masses on its streets are a hungry mob fighting to survive through illegal trafficking and the open prostitution of women and children, a macabre spectacle of humiliation.

This is an outstanding, morally accurate depiction of the Italian people in the aftermath of a lost war, the lugubrious sum of their indignities exposed to the disdainful gaze of the victors.

Rather than an historical inquiry, this book is Malaparte's personal record of appalling social upheaval, his own interpretation of the terrible suffering meted out by fate. FC

'We were clean, tidy and well fed, Jack and I, as we made our way through the midst of the dreadful Neapolitan mob — squalid, dirty, ragged, starving, jostled and insulted in all the languages and dialects of the world by troops of soldiers belonging to the Armies of Liberation, which were drawn from all the races of the earth. The distinction of being the first amongst all the peoples of Europe to be liberated had fallen to the people of Naples; and in celebration of the winning of so well-deserved a prize my poor beloved Neapolitans, after three years of hunger, epidemics and savage air attacks, had accepted gracefully and patriotically the longed-for and coveted honour of playing the part of a conquered people, of singing, clapping, jumping for joy amid the ruins of their houses, unfurling foreign flags which until the day before had been the emblems of their foes, and throwing flowers from their windows on to the heads of the conquerors.' p9

MANZONI
Alessandro

The Betrothed [I Promessi Sposi]

The Betrothed is the 'bible' of Italian literature. Set in seventeenth century Lombardy when Italy was under Spanish rule, it tells the symbolic story of Renzo and Lucia, whose intended wedding is obstructed by the whim of a bullying minor lord, Don Rodrigo. Separated by his peremptory act, they are reunited only after serial misfortunes involving a huge array of characters as many individual stories. The eventual wedding is the triumph of the 'humble' over injustice.

The book was published in its definitive form, after a long gestation period, in 1840 — a critical time when the idea of national unity was making progress in a Lombardy occupied by the Austrians. Among its many merits is its large contribution to the formation of a sense of national identity, which gave the population a spark of hope for a future free from foreign subjugation. It achieved this not only by being a piece of moral education but also by its language. The Italian of *The Betrothed*, an Italian cleansed of regionalisms which rediscovers many of its origins in the dialect of Tuscany, has become a compulsory linguistic point of reference, an event in the history of literature on a par with Dante's *Divine Comedy*. FC

'She was the youngest daughter of Prince ***, a great nobleman of Milan, who could reckon himself among the richest men in the city. But so high an opinion did he hold of his rank, that his wealth seemed only just sufficient, in fact scarcely adequate, to maintain its prestige; and his great preoccupation was to keep what there was all together in perpetuity, so far as lay in his power. History does not tell us how many children he had; all it does is give us to understand that he had destined all the younger children of either sex to the cloister, so as to leave the family fortune intact for the eldest son, whose function it was to perpetuate the family... The unhappy creature of our story was still hidden in her mother's womb when her state in life had already been irrevocably settled. ...On her seeing the light of day, her father the prince, wishing to give her a name which would at once suggest to her the idea of the cloister...called her Gertrude. Dolls dressed as nuns were the first toys to be put into her hands, then holy pictures representing nuns, such presents always being given with warm recommendations to treasure them as something precious, and with a "Lovely, eh?" in a tone of affirmation and interrogation.' p120

Isolina [Isolina, la donna tagliata a pezzi]

At the heart of this book is a murder so atrocious that I had nightmares after reading about it. Dacia Maraini's powerful and sensitively created investigation shows her widening her scope even further as a writer, employing the cinematic description of *The Silent Duchess* (her previous bestseller) married to the left-wing and feminist sympathies of earlier novels such as *The Train* to produce a work of unforgettable impact.

Not a novel, yet unashamed of imaginative speculation, *Isolina* proceeds in a modernist fashion. It displays the way it has been constructed and the reasons for this. The author casts herself as the narrator in order to discover another woman's story, and perhaps finish it for her. She becomes a journalist, trying to discover the truth and finding out how hard that is. She takes swipe after swipe at her subject, coming at it from different angles, following tangles of clues, going off at tangents and into dead-ends.

In the end, she circles back to the beginning: a woman has been murdered, brutally hacked into pieces, and her murderer escapes scot-free. But in the re-telling of this outrage, this tragedy, she lets us put together a pretty good idea of whodunit and why. It's a beautifully reparative book, restoring to the dead woman some dignity and to the dismembered corpse some wholeness. Rather than feeling like a voyeur, the reader becomes a mourner.

In January 1900, a bloody bundle was washed up on the shores of the river Adige in Verona. Inside it were the butchered remains of a young woman. Further bundles provided other parts of her body, including the evidence of her pregnancy. Even later, her head was discovered. The body was identified as that of Isolina Canuti, a young woman living locally, with a reputation for being carefree, generous, pleasure-loving, and, some said, promiscuous. This bad reputation, it turns out, was carefully fostered by key players in the drama, acting as a mask that shielded the perpetrator of her murder.

Maraini's careful and fascinating re-reading of the contemporary newspapers' accounts of the trial that ensued shows how easily injustice could be done to a poor working-class girl when powerful institutions such as the army were involved. Isolina's officer lover protested his innocence of her killing to the last and was believed by nearly everybody.

The book's thrillerish format kept me eagerly reading, despite shudders, to the end. The past came so close: Dacia Maraini, combing present-day Verona for clues, was able to walk where Isolina walked, to stand in the street outside the building where the grisly murder took place, to touch the walls and bridges and shop doors that Isolina touched. There is something very affecting in these accounts of a *real life* that ended much too soon. The experiences and words of poor women are so often unrecorded in the history books, popping up only as examples of transgression in the discourses of the legal process. Yet Isolina's life haunts this book, emerging strongly in the reported anecdotes of her friends. She makes zabaglione for her lover, orders a lace-trimmed bodice from the dressmaker to wear in bed with him, hugs a warming-pan in her lap, confides she doesn't want an abortion.

All these years later, she is listened to again, heard again. But, at the core of the book, we hear her screams, flinch at the terror and the pain. MR

'The cemetery is overflowing with tombstones and flowers. It is hot. The sun has just appeared suddenly from behind white clouds. There are massive tall columns around us. In front of us is a kind of pantheon with the inscription PIUS LACRIMIS. We walk around the gravel paths between ostentatious marble graves covered with flowers. There is much rhetoric amongst the engraved phrases of regret: "sons overwhelmed by the loss of their beloved mother", "sisters longing for their Maria", "husband of the most beloved wife", and so on.

Under glass are yellowed oval portraits of the torsos and heads of women sitting stiffly upright, and men with wild stares. Their dark eyes follow visitors with expressions sometimes ironic, sometimes worried, sometimes ecstatic. There are wrinkled little faces, long beards faded by the damp, children who smile unhappily.' p46

Letters to Marina [Lettere a Marina]

These are letters that will probably never be sent, that tell a tale of love, of rejection and of tenderness mixed with dreams and childhood memories. Letters from the place where Bianca has chosen to hide from her friend, so as not to hear or see her... Letters that arouse the sleeping phantasms of a child of our times; her love for her father, incestual temptation towards the mother, terrifying dreams, family bliss, secret loves, disturbing fears, the hardships of a convent education, the menacing wonders of travelling in far-off Guatemala, lovers, abortions, schooldays, a literary passion for Emily Dickinson, the ever-renewed pleasure in Verdi. Maraini herself said 'I worked for four years on this novel and put in a lot of things that are close to my heart.' A novel composed in a sensual and complex style that is pleasurable to the very end. FC

'Do you remember Alda's solid plates with red borders and the way her teeth would protrude in a quiet withdrawn smile as she offered you food? All the tiresome trivia of life — quarrels traffic money work used to fall away when I arrived at that table set so firmly on the ground with its white tablecloth shining plates and cut-glass decanter filled with water. And the way she cooks everything gently simmering it so that the food is transformed and all the flavours mingle together — the smell of pork fat fried bacon onions lemon verbena all dissolved in the steam rising from the pot. With the powerful hands of someone born and bred in the mountains Alda ladles the red-hot stew on to each plate asking "More? More?" and her shy generous smile tells you that it's not just the stew that is being ladled on to your plate but the most vulnerable part of herself for you to savour appreciatively to the last morsel.' p13

MESSINA
Maria

A House In The Shadows [La Casa Nel Vicolo]

Like Pittigrilli's *Cocaine* (also reviewed in this Babel Guide) this is one of those forgotten-and-rediscovered books; it is also an extraordinary work of art. In a 1920s Sicilian town a petty tyrant of a man wields a blunt and crushing authority over two sisters, immuring them in his cold, selfish little empire, 'the house in the shadows'. Both sisters eventually become his sexual property and he then goes on to victimize his children.

The book has been disinterred in this English translation by a small literary publishing house in Vermont USA partly perhaps for its early feminist message. Paradoxically though *The House in the Shadows* breathes an old-fashioned 'womanly' tone with its flashing glimpses of that mysterious thing, Sicilian emotional life and is much profounder and wider in scope than any propagandistic work could be. RL

'Nicolina brought the pipe to her brother-in-law. He was once again immersed in his papers, frowning but calm... He was a man who never made a mistake, who knew right from wrong. One could only have faith in him, as in the sailor who steers the boat on the open see. It's so good to have faith in someone... And again her heart swelled with boundless admiration for her brother-in-law.

"Here's your pipe," she said meekly. Once more she waited for him to raise his head, in the hope of catching an expression of benevolence in his eyes. Somewhat distressed and humiliated, she sat down next to her sister. She felt a great need to talk, to move, to hear others talking.' p44

MORANTE
Elsa

History [La Storia]

'Storia' is an Italian word which has a double meaning: it denotes 'story', an account of events which may or may not be imaginary, and it is also a word heavy with the burden of the fateful events of mankind's collective past, 'history'. Elsa Morante bases her novel on precisely this twin meaning, and the book alternates the tale of the timid little schoolmistress Ida Ramundo with an ice-cold chronicle of the Second World War, the events of the latter governing those of the former. The war also determines the fate of Ida's son, Useppe. Born of a desperate rape inflicted on Ida by a drunken, homesick German soldier, Useppe's life unfolds amidst the hunger, bombing and destruction that the war produces. This life is tragic, brief and utterly hopeless, and so are those of the people who surround him, all subject to a continual, losing battle to survive: his lively vagabond brother Nino, Davide, an anarchic Jewish character, and Ida herself.

In these people Morante depicts a comfortless humanity, disenfranchised by violence from above and unable to escape the imposition of a macabre destiny. Following the nineteenth-century tradition of the realist, historical novel, she accuses History and Power, the sources of the evil that has invaded the world, and contrasts these with goodness, which is represented by nature, an original state of harmony that man has betrayed. This goodness lives on in the innocents, the victims like Useppe, the mistreated animals that brighten up his childhood, and all those who bear the cross of history. FC

'Frequent visitors, on those lonely days of Useppe's, were the sparrows, who arrived to hop and chatter at the barred window. And since his talent for understanding the language of animals came to him only on certain days, Useppe understood nothing of their chatter except their ordinary cheep cheep cheep. Still it wasn't hard for him to understand that even these guests were looking for a snack. Unfortunately the bread ration was so scant that it was hard for him to find a few leftover crumbs to offer these other starving creatures.' p120

MORAVIA
Alberto

The Conformist [Il Conformista]

After a dark and troubled event in his childhood, a collision between sexuality and violence, the protagonist of *The Conformist* Marcello Clerici wants to have a perfectly normal adult life, one in keeping with established morality. His aim is to become like others, to be swallowed up in the mass of invisible, ordinary people, through strict observance of the rules and conduct that constitute normality. He consequently denies his homosexuality by marrying Giulia, and supports fascism for the sake of that same desire to conform with the majority, going as far as betraying his old university professor and acting as accomplice in his assassination by a fascist death squad. He still doesn't realise that his plan to abide by conventions is no guarantee at all of morality, but rather that abandoning one's true self is fraught with danger and dissolves personal liberty. But only when his true nature frightens him by resurfacing, stronger than his conformism, does he feel lost, and he then recognises that his presumed normality was a vain invention.

The Conformist is a variety of things: the story of a honeymoon in Paris, a crime by the state, the biography of a man, the description of an era and of a society. On reflection though it is clear that this novel is more than anything the description

of a kind of character and a moral behaviour typical of our times. If last century's hero was the rebel, the present century's hero, according to Moravia, is the conformist, the man who wants to merge, to communicate, the man who has chosen to be the same as the rest, and not be himself. One of the great works of European cinema was based on this book, directed by Bernardo Bertolucci. FC

'At this point he felt the need to express his own position in crude, sarcastic words, and said to himself coldly: "If, in fact, Fascism is a failure, if all the blackguards and incompetents and imbeciles in Rome bring the Italian nation to ruin, then I'm nothing but a wretched murderer." But, immediately afterwards he made a mental correction: "And yet, as things are now I couldn't have done otherwise."' p269

Erotic Tales [La Cosa ed altri racconti]

Written late in his career (late in his life in fact), Moravia's *Erotic Tales* seem at first to be exercises in writing that use the erotic as a peg — the exercises of an experienced master-narrator, playfully executed and highly readable. Some of the stories, though, are more serious, shooting questions into the heart of the sexual arena itself. In particular *The Thing*, *The Belt* and *Sign of the Operation* explore the cunningness of perversity in a way that might cause froth to appear at the mouth of those who strive to politicise sexual conduct. Here, in contrast to the nicey-nice world of sexual moralists, we see in Moravia's vision the Sexual Beast who dwells inside freely roaming, driven to follow its obsessions, forever straining at the leash. In as much as recognising the ways in which we connect with one another allows us more liberty to decide our actions than denial ever does, this might be seen as a liberating book. RL

'My hands rummaged among all those soft, vaguely perfumed scraps and, meanwhile,I reflected that rather than dressing themselves as men do, women tend to decorate themselves, and the clothes they wear don't adhere to their bodies but wrap around them in a seductive, mysterious way, concealing what's there, suggesting what isn't there. ...I went on thinking, still rummaging, about the fact that women's clothes don't stay on their bodies like men's do, but move, flutter, puff out, crumple, flap and so on. Or, going to the opposite extreme, they adhere too tightly, and then the female body seems imprisoned in all kinds of elastics, suspenders, girdles, bras and other such harnesses. So, either the fluttering, seductive gauziness, or the tight hermetic sheath.' p181

A Ghost at Noon [Il Disprezzo]

Riccardo Molteni, an impoverished cinema critic, becomes a scriptwriter to ensure a little well-being for his wife Emilia, whom he loves, and who adores him in return. But suddenly, after two years of a happy lovelife, she spurns him, gradually becoming cold and indifferent. Emilia doesn't explain the change in her behaviour but stays enveloped in silence, convinced deep down that the words they might exchange would be banal and useless. It is not so much the occaisionally successful, attentions of the film producer Battista that split the couple as her growing distaste for Riccardo, whose basic weakness of character she has come to understand. Emilia's defection is intolerable for her husband who continues to hope for reconciliation, a fantasy not extinguished even by Emilia's death. Riccardo continues to dream of her, to try and interpret her behaviour and understand her.

This book, an ironic look at the world of cinema and a biting satire on all psychoanalytical pedantry, concludes the Moravian parable of 'conjugal love'. It was made into an powerful film, *Le Mépris*, by Jean-Luc Godard, in the 1960s. FC

'I noticed that she turned her face aside, as if to hide it. But she allowed me to hold her arm; and when I came close to her, so that my side was touching hers, she did not draw back. Then I grew bolder and put my arm around her waist. At last she turned, and I saw that her whole face was wet with tears. "I shall never forgive you," she cried: "never shall I forgive you for having ruined our love. I loved you so much, and I'd never loved anyone but you... and I shall never love anyone else... and you've ruined everything because of your character... We might have been so happy together... and instead of that, it's all quite impossible now. How can I possibly take things for granted? How can I possibly not dislike you?"' p218

The Voyeur [L'Uomo Che Guarda]

This is the story of a 'man who lives through his eyes'. On the one hand it's a wry exploration of the mechanics of a certain dimension of the erotic, with references to the French Decadent poet Mallarmé and to the cult of the Madonna; on the other (and this is probably the true business of the novel), secreted beneath the surface titillation is the domination of the (adult) son by the father.

As the novel progresses one sees that the son, although supposedly a feisty 1968-vintage rebel, is just a shadow-man — and even his shadows are stripped from him. *The Voyeur* is ironic and witty to the point of parody but underneath there is a clever and enlightening essay on psychology, on a phenomenon that is common but rarely commented on. The narrator's submisiveness and his consequent loss of a sense of reality and ability to act on the world are surely as widespread as the existence of overweening authority itself. RL

'Suddenly I think I understand why I hate my father. Because I see he's stronger than I am. Yet at the same time I don't know why he's stronger. Probably if I knew that, I'd stop hating him.' p75

The Woman of Rome [La Romana]

Adriana tells her own story: the story of loss of innocence and subsequent downfall. Her beauty and her natural predisposition for a simple, tranquil life are circumscribed by the corrupt environment that surrounds her and that not even her love for Gino, a driver whom she hopes to marry, can save her from. The discovery that he is already married and has deceived her is a final blow to her natural virtuousness. She becomes a prostitute, the lover of various and varied men: Mino the revolutionary student who she loves, Astarita the fascist functionary who she despises but who loves her,

Sonzogno, the crook whose child she eventually carries. The tales of these three fateful men intertwine with hers but do not truly corrupt her. In fact, in spite of living in what a bourgeois society would consider a scandalous situation, she embodies a more authentic form of innocence and morality which owe more to instinct and nature than to an imposed system of values. The novel closes on an image of hope: Adriana is about to give birth to her child, perhaps into a less unhappy, more straightforward world and one not dominated by violence.

The book lives in its protagonist, the prostitute Adriana, who is undeniably the most vital and sympathetic woman among Moravia's fictional creations, but also one of the most important and intensely emotional characters in contemporary Italian literature. FC

'In any case, I felt so tired that morning, a kind of sensuous laziness, and was less unhappy than I had been the evening before. Mother had gone out very early and I knew she would not come back before midday. So I lingered on in bed, and this was my first pleasure at the beginning of a new phase of my life, which from now on was to be one solely of pleasure. Every day since I was born I had got up in the early hours, and lying idly in bed without doing anything was a real luxury for me. I had never yielded to it, but now I made up my mind to lie in bed whenever I felt like it , and I thought I would act in the same way about all the things I had rejected up till now on the grounds of my poverty and my dreams of a normal family life. I thought how I enjoyed love-making and money and the things money can bring, and I told myself from now on I would never refuse love or money or what money could bring, if I had the chance.' p116

MORAZZONI
Marta

Girl in a Turban [La Ragazza Col Turbante]

Drawn from a series of sixteenth, seventeenth, eighteenth and nineteenth-century scenarios involving characters in middle or old age, the best of these stories really seem to capture fragments of past lives. Some of the historical settings — the sea-voyage of a Flemish art dealer to the Danish countryside, the retreat of the Emperor Charles the Fifth from the Spanish Netherlands to the Estremadura monastery where he chooses to end his life — are fascinating and perfectly, economically evoked. The weaknesses here lie in the problem of using an archaic tone and pace to create atmospheres and a basic unimportance at the heart of some stories. Still, it's 75% a very good book. RL

'By that time Frau Kölner and the children must already have reached the cathedral square, illuminated with the brilliance of daylight. The great door of the church was crammed with the throng which traditionally came crowding to that solemn celebration, pausing on the threshold to exchange greetings and to wait, while within there was a more discreet pattering of feet... Once again Herr Kölner thought nostalgically of the warm, mysterious luminosity of the cathedral, and even had a distinct image in his mind of the faces of the three Church Fathers depicted on Pilgram's famous pulpit emerging from the semi-darkness of the lofty nave.' p145

His Mother's House [Casa Materna]

A book about the kind of lives one *never* sees in the movies, created in an elegant, concise prose by the author and her English translator Emma Rose. These are the lives of the well-off lonely; minutely organized and with all their time (and their emotions) settled, divided up and pre-empted. In this way they keep the affectionless, unpeopled void at bay.

This is a world, existing inside a small but prosperous Norwegian town, of gated houses and trams where a great but serene passion is daily consummated — that of a mature person for her garden. This person, a stern old lady, also loves her son Haakon who, perhaps wisely, has gone to live far away. Somehow, on a visit to Mother, and because of that garden, Haakon, who is a middle-aged virgin, gets a faint but fatal inkling of another kind of life that has passed him by utterly.

The story is told beautifully and delivers that mysterious satisfaction beauty always promises us. RL

'Felice's envy kept him company throughout his long walk on Bergen mountain. So aware was Haakon of her presence that he rediscovered a childhood habit of his: that of holding detailed imaginary conversations with a non-existent companion. In this way he talked to her for a long while, even embarking on a complex discussion, divided into sections and geometrically precise. Questions and answers interwove in perfect alternation with meaningful silences...' p59

Divertimento 1889 [Divertimento 1889]

Convinced that 'we always need fairy stories', Morselli wrote this little tale at the beginning of the 1970s. It's an ingenious and somewhat archaic fable set at the end of the nineteenth century, with the Italian king Umberto the First of Savoy as its central character.

Enticed over the Gotthard pass into Switzerland by what he perceives as an opportunity to turn a quick profit, Umberto sells off a property of his in Monferrato to an eccentric German lady. He sets off incognito with a faithful entourage for the Canton of Uri, and thus begins a light-hearted *Belle Époque* adventure whose farcical verve parades its origins in the French comic playwrights of the nineteenth century and whose 'champagne-like music' imbues the whole narrative with melodic rhythms.

The author abandons himself entirely to his own fertile imagination, categorically excluding any hint of an argument, ever faithful to his project of pure diversion. This is what the book is intended to be and if the reader doesn't succumb, the writer does: 'One person at least, I who wrote it, was diverted'.
FC

'She wore a plain high-necked travel-suit in mauve, the skirt cut so daringly short that it revealed the tops of her boots, with a hint of pleating at the hips, and at the hem the narrowest flounce of Venetian lace; the tight-fitting matching bodice tapered to a point in front and behind; the sole accessory was a little purse slung troubadour-fashion from her waist-band and bumping against her thigh. In bizarre contrast to such elegant simplicity she sported a horsewoman's diminutive glossy top-hat over one ear and trimmed with a white muslin ribbon trailing to her shoulders.'
p61

The Iguana [L'Iguana]

A Count falls for a charming young reptile who lives on an island lost off the Portuguese coast. In its writing and conception the book belongs to the fabulous-modernist mode of Italian literature familiar to readers of Calvino. One discovers here an original way of talking about the human soul, for which the iguana can be read as a metaphor, perhaps. An intriguing book. RL

'The horizon showed only a flush of amber light, yet there was still a leeward glimpse of the low, naked coast of Portugal until, shadow-like, it finally disappeared.' p11

PALANDRI
Enrico

The Way Back [La Via del Ritorno]

A moving, relevant and very *European* book which, as its title suggests, is about a person trying to link up moments of a past scattered by history. The past in question is that of a young man growing up in the late 1960s in a hyper-politicised Italy. It is also his past as a child brought up by a Jewish mother whose own past was violently interrupted in the Warsaw of September 1939, as the government crumbled and the roads out of the city filled with refugees. The protagonist, an Italian doctor who lives in London, tries to understand what his identity might be through the eyes of his Scottish lover and his immigrant parents, who suffer from that spiritually deadly complaint, nostalgia.

The Way Back is a tender essay on the inner life of the New Europe, born in dreams and sired by nightmares, on our common mother, with her necessary or convenient amnesias, on an Italy 'which is painfully mine'. Palandri is already (in 1990) writing after the fall of Communism, the definitive end of World War Two, and therefore has an overview which allows him both to join up the experience of different moments in Europe's history and to unite this history with that of other places: on a train we see Europeans alongside Africans and Asians, all of them refugees of sorts, 'fleeing from those years, thrown together in panic and anxious over any sort of future'.

Although a book about ordinary Italians, *The Way Back* is written with the sharpened and wider consciousness of the exile and has something to say to all Europeans. RL

'The bar was packed with Italians...To be there, however successful they had been in fitting in, was the result of a defeat. It meant not to have found work at home, to have dreamt too much of some other place, to have problems with the law, their family, their friends, or their city, not to have loved enough the vine-coloured hills from which they came, the blue sea and the cement courtyards, not to have been able to hold on to what they had.' p125

PAPINI
Giovanni

The Failure [Un Uomo Finito]

Papini was one of the most talked-about and controversial intellectuals of the first two decades of this century. The *grand provocateur* of Florentine culture and founder, with Prezzolini, of *La Voce*, the magazine that marked a unique and fervent period in literature, Papini's life epitomizes that of a whole generation about to enter the deadly arena of the First World War. He was the pioneer, the reckless agitator of a muddled ideology of anti-bourgeois rebellion, but also the poet singing of a return to an archaic and simple scale of life.

The Failure, an autobiography that Papini published in 1912 when he was just thirty years old, charts the first period of his life, from his childhood to the symbolic moment when he reaches maturity. It has the readability of an epoch-making document and is a comprehensive testament to the idealistic exasperation of certain intellectuals that would, only a short while later, drive some of them to subscribe blindly to Italy's ghastly nationalist and fascist movements. FC

'The country that appeals to me is *my own* country Tuscany, where I learnt to breathe and to think; a poor, grey, bare, circumscribed region, lacking luxuriance and bright colours, lacking perfume and pagan garlands, yet so intimate, so friendly, so well suited to sensitive natures, to the hermit mind. A monkish, Franciscan country, rude and black, where one is conscious of the skeleton of stone beneath the green sod, where the great, dark, lonely hills rise suddenly as if threatening the peaceful, fertile valleys at their base. The sentimental country of my childhood this, the lean, dry Tuscan country, with its granite, its honest, common flowers, its bold cypresses and sturdy oaks and rough brambles- how much more beautiful it has seemed to me than the famed regions of the south, with their palms, their oranges and prickly pears, their white dust and fierce summer!' pp48-49

PARISE
Goffredo

The Boss [Il Padrone]

In *The Boss* Parise was trying to write a fable about the mental and psychological exploitation of man in late industrial society. He tries to go beyond Marx's formula of economic exploitation and explore the effect on a man's heart and soul of being a cog in the machinery of capitalism. In an interview Parise himself said 'My man-object in *The Boss* is no longer a tradeable item, but is already absolute property, who "morally" releases the master from the realm of business and raises him to the much more ambitious heights of theology.' FC

PASOLINI
Pier Paolo

The Ragazzi [I Ragazzi]

The Ragazzi ('the lads') is a unique, cruel but convincing picture of post-war Italy seen from the bottom. The young Pasolini had found himself exiled to the outskirts of Rome after a politico-sexual scandal back home in the rural and conservative North-Eastern province of Friuli. The book kicks off with a pair of delinquents stealing pennies from a blind beggar; its itinerary continues with visits to brothels, reminiscences of nights spent under the Tiber bridges of Ponte Sisto and Ponte Garibaldi, days spent in the Regina Coeli ('Queen of Heaven') prison and in the terminal wards of hospitals. As ever in Pasolini's work there is a magnificent, highly sexual sense of human vitality. RL

'The heat...was like a warm hand laid on the light breeze, on the yellowish walls of the district...on the broken sidewalks and along colossal ruined walls with lines of hovels at their bases. There were young men racing on their motor scooters, Lambrettas, Ducatis, or Mondials, half-crocked, their greasy jumpers open on their hairy chests, or else dressed to kill as if they'd just stepped out of a show-window on the Piazza Vittorio. There was a great encirclement of Rome and of the countryside around about on the part of hundreds of thousands of human beings, swarming among their blocks of dwellings, their squatters' shacks, or their skyscrapers.' p195

A Violent Life [Una Vita Violenta]

When it appeared in 1959, *UnaVitaViolenta* was immediately acclaimed for its depiction of a highly *un*picturesque life of poverty and for Pasolini's rendition of the strange new dialect born in the Roman shanty-towns. With its starveling boy prostitutes and venomously violent fascist youths, it's an extraordinary portrait — half-novel and half-documentary, a collection of 'episodes' rather than short stories — of people on the edge of the city, of the economy, of politics. RL

'At the corner of the bridge, above him, under a kind of white column like a tombstone, two whores were standing, crossly, one in a red topcoat, the other, testy and rumpled, wearing a black sweater. Both were squat, with bellies that made them look pregnant, short fat legs, black, hairy faces, low foreheads like monkeys. They were swinging their purses.' p18

A Dream of Something [Il Sogno di una Cosa]

The 'dream' is communism, with which Pasolini, as an artist, a genuine, freethinking radical and practising homosexual, had a very difficult relationship. The book returns to his youth in the peasant world of Friuli in North-East Italy. With tender lyricism he recounts its life of dances, fairs and wine-drunken expeditions. In the title story a small group of left-wing peasant youths set out for neighbouring Yugoslavia to taste for themselves the benefits of communist rule. The hungry, hopeless time they have there supplies an interesting and realistic vignette of post-war life.

To read the book today is to inhale the convivial beauty of Italian peasant life; the beauty of a world swallowed up by its transformation into a consumer society, a process Pasolini bitterly lamented. RL

'It was the evening of Epiphany and it was an evening of great excitement in the Faedis' byre among the women who were there spinning.

There was a special air of merriment, partly because they had visitors — a young wife and the Owl, that chatterbox with her little girl's voice which no one could silence, who had come from nearby cottages. For two hours there was nothing but talk, laughter, noise, so much so that although the little boys might have been dying of sleep they did not intend to lose a word of this evening of merriment.' p106

Theorem [Teorema]

Theorem is a late work, produced when Pasolini was reaching the height of his fame as a unique film-maker (*Theorem* is also the title of a film he made while writing this book). It's an important book because in it Pasolini coherently demonstrates his anger, his understanding of the emptiness and spiritual corruption of consumer society, particularly the unjust Italian one in which 'equality' means no more than the right to consume. It's also very interesting from a structural point of view; it's not the film script presented as a book one might expect but rather a 'modernist literary artefact' that is neither novel nor essay. Maybe this is the future of the book as an art form. RL

'She too loses herself down the silent street where the guest was lost; she too is swallowed up by that desolate and arrogant stage-set of houses of the rich for whom it is a duty to give no sign of life.

The set alone remains — the index of an unreality which, in concrete terms, takes the form of a district of the dead, whose stones, whose cement, whose trees are a spectacle, motionless under the sun, which by its presence causes pain and offence.' p135

Roman Nights & Other Stories [A selection from Ali dagli Occhi Azzurri]

These are five stories, set in Rome and Paris, selected mainly from one of Pasolini's richest books, the collection *Ali dagli Occhi Azzurri* published in 1965. One could say that here Pasolini was at his height as a prose writer, writing with a kind of merciless lucidity not equaled before or since. He manages in *A Rustic Story* for instance to write in a savagely ironic tone without ever seeming arrogant or uncaring about his protagonists. The book reveals a harsh and unsentimental canvas of rent boys, illegal immigrants and street children.

This is a very different Pasolinian world to the spiritual and philosophical preoccupations of his films such as *The Gospel according to Saint Matthew* and *Theorem* or the wry sensuality in *Canterbury Tales* or *Decameron*. The mystery is how did one artist achieve so much in the separate fields of poetry, prose and the cinema? The breadth of Pasolini's work puts him in a very rare category of 'cultural genius' and this collection, originally published by the excellent American Marlboro Press and now also in Quartet, is a fitting tribute. RL

'On winter evenings, when a vein of warmth spreads by flattening itself on surfaces that smell of washed and reheated rags, of old iron on which the sun, scrubbed by the wind, beats without warning — or else a mood flat as a metal pan reflects from a country sky threadlike laminae that attach themselves to serrated edges and to walls — orange-coloured fibres are lighted over the square cobblestones used to pave the streets...with a layer of hard dust, almost abstract, and discharging a filth by which feelings are more infected than bodies.' p55 *A Night On The Tram*

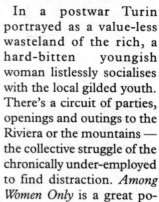

PAVESE
Cesare
Among Women Only [Tra Donne Sole]

In a postwar Turin portrayed as a value-less wasteland of the rich, a hard-bitten youngish woman listlessly socialises with the local gilded youth. There's a circuit of parties, openings and outings to the Riviera or the mountains — the collective struggle of the chronically under-employed to find distraction. *Among Women Only* is a great polemic against vacuousness, written with a bitter edge that really illuminates this world. Pavese is utterly economical in the choice and succession of images for his narrative and the brush-strokes he uses for his characters. A masterpiece by one of Italy's truly great modern authors. RL

'There were paintings and small statues on the wall; I passed them up and looked at Nene instead, who, in her usual rags, laughed continuously, sprawled across a chair, crossing and uncrossing her legs, while a waiter lighted her cigarette from behind.'
p212

The Devil in the Hills [Diavolo Sulle Colline, La Bella Estate]

In *The Devil in the Hills* Pavese contrasts the city (post-war Turin) with a countryside still partly inhabited by 'real folks' but already becoming a playground for the Northern Italian idle rich who both fascinated and appalled him. As in *Among Women Only,* he contrasts upwardly mobile, hard-working youths with distracted, spoilt, rich kids. There's a dialogue too between various moral codes personified by different characters: we have a highly observant Catholic maiden aunt full of priest-speak, a millionaire's son who drifts rudderless between cocaine, adultery and suicide and a narrator who seems to operate an even more tiresome compromise between these two extremes.

Especially enjoyable is Pavese's celebration of physicality, of the human body in the sunlight or in water, the body close to nature — different from today's exercise-culture which seems to involve so much in the way of machinery, special outfits, food-supplements and so on. Pavese's vision, like that of Albert Camus or even D.H.Lawrence, reflects nature in a less mediated way. RL

'That sun bath had become almost a vice, though by now we were tanned all over. On the first Sunday we didn't go down but spent the noon hour in front of the church in the festive crowd, listening to Mass from the doorway amid a confusion of boys, organ music, and bells. But I greatly missed being naked and flattened out between the earth and the sun...

To Pieretto, who was looking sardonically at Oreste's neck, I whispered: "Can you imagine these people naked in the sun like us?"'
p325

The Moon and the Bonfire [La Luna e il Falò]

Set in an impoverished corner of the Piedmontese country-side, this is the *Pastorale* of a writer who spent most of his adult life in industrial Turin. It describes a type of desperate rural poverty now rare in Europe but still common in the Third World: conditions that drove thousands of people to emigrate or even commit suicide.

The social commentary implicit in such a setting led early critics to see the book as a piece of political fiction, but the contemporary reader might be more struck by the sense of alienation that runs through the story. Anguilla ('The Eel'), the narrator, is a man with no family and no friends who leaves home in the late 1920s hoping to return one day as a 'somebody', but finds himself always unable to participate in the intimacy of life. When he does return his home has become unrecognisable, mauled by war and social upheaval.

While the landscape and the atmosphere through which Anguilla moves are common to many European books of the late 1940s and early 1950s, the intensity of Pavese's tone and narrative marks *The Moon and the Bonfire* out. Some of this intensity is found in his portrayal of women, who often seem the more complete and convincing characters in Italian fiction. The novel is haunted by the three sisters Silvia, Irene and Santina, who torment Anguilla with a beauty and grace which lies far beyond his reach.

Although the women's lives here all end tragically, there is a sense that they have all at least *lived*, felt and suffered whereas Anguilla the exile, whether as a boy in Italy, away in California seeking his fortune or returned home, always stands outside, his heart permanently frozen through the emotional and material hardship he has endured. RL

'Once upon a time I'd had a longing within me (one morning in a bar in San Diego I nearly went mad with it) to come out on to the main road, to push open the iron gate between the pine and the lime trees at the corner, to hear the voices and the laughter and the hens and say, "Here I am, I've come back," watching their bewildered faces — the farmhands, the women, the dog, the old man and the grey eyes and the brown eyes of the girls would have recognised me from the terrace — it was a longing I'd never get rid of now.' p80

Summer Storm [Racconti di Cesare Pavese]

In this early and particularly revealing collection of stories by a man who is now seen as one of the greatest Italian writers of the century, Pavese's unafraid, acid-strong gaze burns through social appearances to reveal the callousness of much human behaviour, and does so with an honesty that is empowering rather than depressing.

In *The Evil Eye* an ordinary man who is neither handsome, powerful, clever nor well-connected is treated like a dog. In *Misogyny* a couple literally appear out of the fog, young, in desperate trouble, feverish and anguished; no explanation is given, there is just a superb *malaise*. *Summer Storm* has a pair of low-lifers who suddenly turn nasty, characters reminiscent of many of those in Pasolini's *A Violent Life*.

The extraordinary story *The Idol* shows a besotted lover waiting for the object of his desire outside the brothel where she, apparently willingly, works while he torments himself with thoughts of her serving her clients. There is something particularly awful and convincing about the characters in this story. Part of the effect comes from the subtle way Pavese conveys the passing of time, making us perceive it through the protagonist's individual consciousness — a talent he shares with Flaubert, Conrad and Joyce.

The Family might offer insights into Pavese the man, and perhaps into other intellectual types as well, the kind of people who enjoy their solitude more than they regret not being in company. Like much of his writing, it contains terrifically effective portraits of women characters. Pavese was both fascinated and jealous of women's sociability and seems to have suffered from as well as enjoyed his intellectual solitude. He painted women in the light of his resentful fascination, but there is also an astonishing empathy — perhaps he understood women too well to get along with them. RL

'One morning she unexpectedly asked to see my room and put it tidy for me. Nervously I took her up the old, gloomy staircase and threw open the window as soon as we were inside. With fresh air and light there came a new awareness. On the floor lay my gaping suitcase near the half-opened cupboard, and a pile of old catalogues from my firm. The dirty coffee cups on the side table and the untouched bed were just as I had seen but scarcely noticed as I went out a little while ago. Mina walked over to me and kissed me. Even today, when it's all over, I still tremble at the memory of the pure, firm sweetness of her hidden body. All the time Mina gazed at me with her limpid eyes, caressing my spine. There was a fresh atmosphere about it all, such as I have never known since.' *The Idol* p27

Festival Night [Notte di Festa]

The first story here, *Land of Exile*, is about the impotence of the exile, written not long after Pavese's own period of juridical exile for writing articles against the fascist government. The short piece *Wedding Trip*, in which a man crushes his wife's spirit with meanness, is reminiscent of George Orwell's preoccupation with the brutalising psychological effects of poverty and the drying-up of emotional generosity — a subject re-examined in the story *Suicide*s.

Friends captures the feel of small-town life in describing a band of youths growing up together, a kind of worn-in common experience of mutual boredom mixed with mutual sympathy. One of the band enters into a claustrophobic marriage with a local girl while another goes off to 'adventures' in Ethiopia (which Italy invaded in the 1930s) and returns to drink up his pay. *Friends* has the concreteness that characterises most of Pavese's work, a quality not so common in writing from Latin countries, which tend towards more lyrical and rhetorical literary traditions.

Gaol Birds presents Concia, a wonderfully betraying woman who is either an enormous stereotype or a magnificent archetype. In *The Cornfield* Pavese drums up a novel's-worth of atmosphere as he rolls out two of his big themes: the rejection of peasant life by the young and the falsity of lovers. The way he works these two themes is a great achievement, as he himself wrote, 'The style of the twentieth century expresses but does not explain...It is a never-ending revelation of inner life'. RL

'In the dead of night she was awakened by footsteps outside the door and the sound of heavy breathing. A dog, perhaps? Or a drunk? Terror and uncertainty kept her trembling on the sofa, her eyes starting open as she heard a coming and going, a creaking. Could it be the wind? Her heart felt numb with horror and shame at having to sleep in a low kitchen like a peasant girl, behind a door by the road, at the mercy of every passer-by....She was terrified in case the door was not properly shut; even worse was her dread of anyone seeing the sink in the corner with its constant dripping. She screwed up her eyes and tried to sleep. *The Cornfield* p208

This Business of Living. A Diary 1935-1950 [Quel Mestiere di Vivere]

(This review breaks the rules of the Babel Guide; this book is neither in print nor a work of fiction – we wanted to introduce it to our readers anyway.) This Business of Living is Pavese's dialogue with himself and his dialogue with us, written in the years of his greatest achievements as a writer and ending with his suicide. A hard review to write because I've been reading this book for nearly 20 years, keeping it on my bedside table, alongside Albert Camus' *Notebooks*. Part of the attraction is that this small book touches on such a huge range of topics; on the books Pavese himself read and commented on; on moral and philosophical issues he was concerned with as well as his continual and sometimes tortured self-analysis. There is present here the wide world of an active, energetic intellectual, a man bent on critically understanding everything that comes before him. *This Business of Living* is the mirror of a personality that transcends the limitations of most human lives; the personality of a genius.

In Pavese one sees the two aspects of the 20th century creative genius; the being very *close* to the culture or world one springs from and the state of feeling far outside of it. Pavese, who describes so intimately the thoughts and feelings of others was famously a loner, a non-conformist, an awkward character, living at a great distance from other people and suffering for that. Yet his two greatest works of fiction *The Moon and the Bonfire* and *Among Women Only,* show his closeness to things, to a landscape and to the social beat of a great city respectively — Pavese lived in great intimacy with his beloved places, rather like Pasolini who wrote 'I spend the greater part of my life beyond the edges of the city... I love life with such violence and such intensity that no good can come of it. I am speaking of the physical side of life: the sun, the grass, youth. It is an addiction more terrible than cocaine. It doesn't cost anything, and it is available in vast quantities...how it will all end, I don't know.' (quoted in S.Pacifici *From Verisimo to Existentialism* London 1969)

A diary of such a great writer, a writer with such a fierce connection with life, is an unfathomably rich work that one can enter again and again always finding more. It is also shows that a diary can be a very complex work of art, one that uses a very basic narrative logic, the march of time itself. Within that straightforward structure anything can happen as the connections between entries are made only by the mental structure of the diary's author, and with the passage of time.

Although completed almost 50 years ago, *This Business of Living* can be considered today as one of the most contemporary works translated from Italian into English. RL

5th March 1939

'...only gradually do we come to understand that our way of life is our own creation; in all its minute ramifications it is the expression of our experience. The troubles of young people are born of the impossibility of making their own experience coincide with the broad, stylized impression they have gained of the world. Any profession, any social status, seems to a young man remote and unattainable, until, little by little, he has created his own status and profession — totally different, in their slow, inner growth, from the clumsy vision he imagined and dreaded. But then he is a man.' p82

PAZZI
Roberto

Searching For The Emperor [Cercando L'Imperatore]

This is an historical novel about the final days of the Russian Royal family, imprisoned by the Bolsheviks shortly before their assassination. As they edge toward the hour of reckoning a last loyal regiment picks its way across Siberia to rescue them. Fluttering at the edge of the quietly disintegrating regiment and the doomed family are fragments of other worlds: hunters of the Taiga forest, the ghost of Rasputin, an ancient, self-confident peasant civilisation, harried Jews, enclosed Russian Orthodox nuns...

It *should* all be more interesting than it actually is, given its complex, thought-provoking themes: the willingness of men to embrace delusion in difficult times, the relationship of a disciplined organisation like the army to a culture of forest hunters... There's a sentimental view of Tsarism here that could convince only the historically ignorant. But there are wonderful moments and images: the Tsarina's sister, a lively woman trapped inside Imperial mummery, who 'could lie so well to herself she forgot she was inventing half her life'; the lonely Tsarevich's childish fantasy of a companion who 'followed him with hesitant, troubled steps, as though unaware of him waiting for her ahead, as if not seeing him'; and the peasant soldiers far from their villages and too long in the Tsar's army. RL

'...they dreamt of returning to their isbas, to sleep above the stove, to lay in peat during the summer and cook and chat around the fire in winter, waiting for spring. The fields were waiting for them, so thick with wheat every summer that it was difficult to see how one pair of arms could reap all that gold from the earth blessed by God.' p149

PETRIGNANI
Sandra

Interview: The Toy Catalogue [Il Catalogo dei Giocattoli]

Born in 1952, Sandra Petrignani is one of Italy's 'giovani scrittori' or young writers of the 1980s and 1990s, many of whom were originally promoted by Rome's adventurous Theoria publishing house and now write for the Milanese literary magazine Panta. They were perhaps the first post-war generation to escape the shadow of literary giants such as Alberto Moravia and Cesare Pavese. Petrignani's book The Toy Catalogue *reads partly as a mock-encyclopaedic study of toys and games and partly as a memoir of childhood; it also hints at the overspill of childhood sensations into the lives of adults, their sexuality and style of behaviour, thus serving as psychological self-exploration. She was interviewed for Babel in London in 1990.*

BABEL: I remember looking for the first time at the contents page of *The Toy Catalogue*. In one hundred and thirty pages there are sixty-five chapters: *Balloons, Building Blocks, The Unknockdownable Man* and so on. Then my eye picked out *View Master* and reading that chapter I had a clear mental snapshot of that clunky brown thing with the picture wheels — I was tugged into the forgotten past of childhood with its sharp focus and vivid colours. How did you manage to get that evocative charge in your book?

PETRIGNANI: With Proust's method of 'involuntary memory', the famous madeleine....I gathered up and played around with toys. I spread them over my desk, I had little

wooden horses, a rag doll, toy cars and so on. I'd go and borrow my son Guido's toys, he was about five then, and he'd angrily come looking for them. Then I remember getting some of those big old glass marbles they don't make anymore, so today's children don't play with them, but Guido knew of course they were toys so he was convinced they were his property. There was a big tussle over that. Also friends brought me toys, things like wooden animals in an old-fashioned style and still being made up in the mountains.

BABEL: *L'Europeo* magazine called the book 'an extraordinary achievement of memory' that 'restores to us the magical territory of play.' And everyone I know who's read it here has referred to this depth of memory.

PETRIGNANI: Something that happened with *The Toy Catalogue* was that although I thought I'd had an unhappy childhood, after writing the book I realised it wasn't true. I got back to the nice parts of being a child. I realised it's terribly easy to lay a sadness that comes later over those years. When you touch the involuntary memories then all those pleasurable experiences return.

'Here's a word (*Il Carillon* or Music Box) that makes no mystery about what it means, the very sound of it is music. The ballerina with the white tutu awakes from her imprisonment inside the lacquered box. She dances on red velvet before the mirror set into the lid. The waltz is over, she comes to a halt. With her arm so gracefully arched, she waits at the ready, not knowing whether she should dance on or go back to sleep. Hair black as ebony, lips red as blood, her prince is the hand that turns the key to wind the mechanism. Merely opening the box isn't enough, the ballerina gets to her feet but just stands there, paralysed by the silence. Only the music can give her life. The melody drives her around and around in an infinite pirouette. A little click every three turns and she changes direction. Her loneliness is devastating.' p57 *The Music Box*

PIRANDELLO
Luigi
One, None and a Hundred Thousand [Uno, Nessuno e Centomila]

Pirandello's last novel, first published in 1927, is the work of his that most elucidates his thought. The story revolves around Vitangelo Moscarda, a man from the provinces who is suddenly struck by the realisation that the nature of man is not *essence* but *appearance*: he doesn't have *one* personality but rather the hundred thousand that others discern in him — hence the title. He falls into incessant speculation, attempting to give his life a new meaning. Everyone else takes him for a madman, his wife leaves him and he gets shut up in a mental hospital where he is free to be no-one and everyone at the same time, as every second he dies and is reborn with a new face and without memories. There he lives in tranquillity, no longer a man but earth, air, cloud and wind.

The drama of identity into which Moscarda is plunged is a constant theme in Pirandello's writing. Here, the impossibility of simply *being* precipitates his protagonist into a search for self-annihilation, a conscious dissolution of his own personality. FC

'The home stands in the country, in a lovely spot. I go out every morning, at dawn, because now I want to keep my spirit like this, fresh with dawn, with all things as they are first discovered, that still smack of the raw night, before the sun dries their moist respiration and dazzles them.' p160

Notebooks of Seration Gubbio [Quaderni di Seration Gubbio]

Written in the first person, the novel takes the form of the diary of an imperturbable film camera-man who has the job of fixing deceiving images of a life which, in reality, changes from moment to moment. Seration has an almost sacred devotion to his work and isn't distracted even when he finds himself filming a scene in which imitation becomes reality as an actor kills an actress out of jealousy as she acts alongside him. The resulting trauma turns him mute and shuts him inside a silence from which even a woman's love can't free him. He has, in effect, become a prisoner of the silent monologue which he captures with his movie camera, unchangeable, excluded from the constant flux of life.

The novel is unique in Pirandello's oeuvre because of the story's location. The world of the cinema is here the symbol of a society in disintegration, subjected to the rule of the utilitarian and empty of all human values; a society in which the machine is beginning to take man over, replacing his needs and feelings with the impersonal precision of technique. This is the process that is really engulfing Seration and reducing him to silence. FC

'I am here. I serve my machine, in so far as I turn the handle so that it may eat. But my soul does not serve me. My hand serves me, that is to say serves the machine. The human soul for food, life for food, you must supply gentlemen, to the machine whose handle I turn.... Already my eyes and ears too, from force of habit are beginning to see and hear everything in the guise of this rapid, quivering, ticking mechanical reproduction.' p10

PITIGRILLI

Cocaine [Cocaina]

Pitigrilli heads the list of forgotten writers whose disappearance from memory was the result of excessive fame in their own time, in this case the 1920s and 30s. Pitigrilli's rediscovery today is due to a man with a heroic capacity for scavenging the refuse heap of minor literature: Umberto Eco. He was the one to realise that this obscure purveyor of forbidden fruit was actually a writer who was 'pleasurable, savoursome and quick, full of fireworks' and above all 'pure author'. And in fact one does get that impression reading this book with its unmistakably D'Annunzian atmosphere, its potently decadent style broken by flashes of irony and disenchantment and its story that exhales an open-minded, worldly-wise frivolity.

The main character, a successful young journalist called Tito, is frustrated by small-town snobbery, leaves for Paris and discovers there the way to indulge in 'the sweet voluntary death that each of us in different tones and with different words desires': *cocaine.* From the irresistibly seductive drug his passion stretches to a woman who takes on in his eyes a thousand qualities, creating a dependency he cannot escape — thus he is doubly poisoned. But the real evil is a perverse form of passion, of loving. Maud's libertine nature excites his jealousy, a desire to possess her that she won't submit to not only because she is emancipated but also because she, like him, comes from an environment without values, in a state of moral decomposition.

The book justifies the attention of a contemporary reader; it's a highly enjoyable expedition into a world that is pure surface, sterile aestheticism. Here we move through smoky rooms, amongst Oriental fabrics in an atmosphere of absolute luxuriousness and languor blown apart from time to time by Pitigrilli's sardonic comments. FC

'What an intelligent woman, he said to himself. With what purity and simplicity she described to me how it happened that first time. It was hot, there was a man available, she was excited, she wanted him, she gave herself to him without making a noise, without pretending. Other women say: The man was a coward, I was a child, I knew nothing, I understood nothing, he took advantage of me. Or: He gave me something to drink, I don't know what and I went to sleep. When I woke up... Or they say: My mother was dying, we had no money for medicine, or the doctor, or even a coffin.... And they say: Oh, if only I'd known, oh, the revulsion, the hatred I feel for that man and the loathing I feel for myself.

Instead (Tito went on to himself) this delicious Maud talks about the first time as she would about her first communion, if that were worth talking about. She attaches no importance to that physical episode, that superficial incident, that harmless, simple, quiet event about which poets, moralists, judges at all times and in all ages have made such a fuss. That minor act of nervous release that had led to savage injustices and idiotic philosophical outpourings, in the name of morality; that natural interplay of two bodies that appears so different depending on whether it happens before or after a carriage ride to the town hall, and is considered decent and honourable if it is done in one bed and wicked if it done in another.' pp87–88

PRATOLINI
Vasco

Family Chronicle [Cronaca Familiare]

This intensely lyrical work emerged from a real and painful experience and Pratolini avoids all invention, staying close to the actual story of his relationship with his younger brother Ferruccio, who died young through illness. Their family's economic situation forced the brothers to grow up separately — the author in the harsh streets of a city *quartiere*, Ferrucio within the walls of a well-off household — and when they eventually met again they found each other very changed. Pratolini was puzzled by the solitary and timid existence of his brother, which contrasted with his own vital, open and companionable life. But their blood relationship kindled a desire in both to get to know each other again in spite of all the obstacles, misunderstandings and embarrassments that separation had thrown their way. One such obstacle was Ferruccio's illness; his youth was accelerated and then extinguished by an incurable disease. In the face of this the author tries to take stock of the whole mysterious human quality of his brother.

First published in 1947, this is a kind of intimate report in which the writer appears vulnerable and intent only on articulating, by using his gift for writing, an appreciation of another person, something that was denied him while that person was alive. FC

'This book is not a work of the imagination. It is the writer's dialogue with his dead brother. The writer in writing it is seeking consolation and nothing else. He suffers from the guilty knowledge of having barely appreciated the spiritual qualities of his brother and then too late. These pages can be only a sterile expiation.' (*from the author's preface*)

PRESSBURGER
Giorgio & Nicola

The Law of White Spaces [Legge Degli Spazi Bianchi]

These five stories, set mainly in the poverty-stricken, sometimes chaotic Budapest of before and just after World War Two, form a series of reflections on illness and its resonances in our feelings. This is an unusual theme for literature and one that gives the stories a fresh, revelatory force.

The title piece shows a doctor afflicted with a disease that makes his memory slip away from him literally word by word until he comes to believe that meaning really resides not in words but in the white spaces between words... The strange tale *Vera* illustrates a similar disturbance of outer and inner worlds. As in much of Pressburger's writing, a lot of the main action takes place out of frame. In this sense Pressburger's work is like that of S.Y.Agnon, another Jewish writer also originally from Mitteleuropa. Agnon was described as having 'a deliberately restrained tone of narration'. This restraint, this delicacy in the face of individual tragedy and the general loss of war and social dislocation also marks Pressburger's tone. Both writers' work is set against the background of a world that no longer exists; their writing and their memories are, practically speaking, all that remains of it. Perhaps it is this great sadness, indirectly reflected in their stories, that makes the stories more than they appear to be at first glance. RL

'He was a swift worker; no one else could set as many ens per hour as he could. Typographical errors were unknown to him. He could decipher the most garbled manuscripts. And no spelling mistake ever escaped him, no matter how deeply buried in the work of some poet or novelist. He would sit at his machine for thirteen, fourteen hours a day. With his pliers he would pull the tiny pieces of lead, each one embossed with a letter, from the packed wooden cases, and from there slide them into position in lines of type. The thoughts enclosed in each symbol by his own two hands danced before his eyes; and no messages born in dark rooms would find their way in the hands of other people into sumptuous buildings.' p155

The Green Elephant, The [L'Elefante verde]

Like *Homage to the Eighth District* and *The Law of White Spaces* by the Pressburgers this book emerges from memories of a poor Jewish Budapest in the period from the end of the First World War to the end of the second — which doesn't at all convey that behind its simple storytelling is a profound and rather magical reflection on life and on the burden or gift of parental expectations.

This charming novella, told mainly through a child's eyes, is secretly an essay on a strand that has deeply marked exceptional Jews throughout the last few centuries; the messianic, utopian, far-seeing urge that often possesses them; something born out of the combination of the notion of a Chosen People, their relative sophistication in a world of ignorant peasants and feckless aristocrats and the actual limitation on what Jews were allowed to do in a universe of hostility and discrimination. A yearning for a better, holier, richer, wider life thus became deeply ingrained and the dream of the Green Elephant that is the keynote of this book seems to be a beautiful literary reflection of the rich and felicitously mad idea many Jews have had that the world will/can/must change for the better.

The writing of *The Green Elephant* is in a peculiarly exalted vein and as sweet and pungent as a *heimishe* pickled cucumber and well reflected by the marvellous jacket design by Graham Peake. Our glimpse into District Eight develops into a *Kaddish* (the Jewish prayer for the dead) for Europe's Lost Tribe, an elegiac, fanciful and beautiful tribute. A book of twins, written by twins and a very honest parable about the desire *not* to be chosen of the exceptional and gifted personality trying to resist the responsibility that the free gift of exceptional intelligence, subtlety or beauty demands of its bearer.

'The young couple went to live in Kun Street, near the Teleky market, in a single alley-like room which stretched from the railings overlooking the courtyard on the inside of the house to the external wall on the other side, into which was set the only window. It was a poor dwelling: the only thing that made it bearable was the knowledge that the other Jews of the Eighth District were no better off. The wedding bed was a present from Rachel's mother. There was little else in the way of furniture: a chest of drawers, a table, one or two chairs and a radio with a green-lit dial completed the set-up. A cupboard in the middle of the room gave them somewhere to store their kitchen utensils. The kitchen stove just sat inside the door; its red glow lit up the room in the cold winter evenings as the couple rested after a long day's work.' p47

Brothers [Fratelli]

An old house, with two brothers who are united in a relationship which goes well beyond the family tie and seems to constitute a way of life for them both, basing itself on the sickness of the one and the health of the other. But if this is the scenario and the brothers the dramatis personae that play it out then in fact, after a few pages, all the details seem to blur and the image of the one is mirrored in the other, apparent normality is refracted in sickness and the helper discovers himself in the one he helps. Only the act of writing provides any lucidity in this tangled situation, this infinite series of mirrors.

A book which, despite a very lean narrative thread, grips and enwraps the reader, dragging him into a theatre full of lamenting voices, repeated actions, wheezing breaths, recreating the image of that obscure, difficult variety of love, we call 'fraternal'. FC

'I can't imagine any territory more intimately my own, any realm where I have more right to boast of exclusive ownership, any space where I may enter and exit more easily, without my brother's knowledge...writing builds around me potential universes, an alternative to the reality which frightens me but where I am forced to remain.' pp111-112

Childhood of Nivasio Dolcemare [Infanzia di Nivasio Dolcemare]

The author's name is hidden anagramatically in the protagonist's first name; 'Dolcemare' is the mythic and sacred place where his childhood was lived, the marine landscape of Greece. But the author's name is itself a borrowed one, adopted to escape the burdensome kinship of an illustrious brother, the painter Giorgio de Chirico. The play on names is full of significance for Savinio; also for the young Nivasio, who is surrounded by characters whose names sound like distorted words, satirical and suggestive: Father Visanio (another play on Savinio), Signora Trigolina ('Big Mullet'), Doctor Naso ('Nose')...It is through these names that we see the child's struggle against the adult state, his rejection of its ways and its ridiculous complacency which he challenges by his fantastic, metaphysical adventures.

Childhood of Nivasio Dolcemare is a record of the anxieties of childhood sexuality, its death-wish and prepubescent *angst*; childhood recorded neither as comedy nor drama but as a tragedy of sacrifice and self-abasement that the language turns into a play on words. It is also an exemplary tale of suffering, lack of understanding, solitude and sensuality, a hangar full of luminous and illusory pleasures in which the boy Nivasio incubates his scorn for the adult world, his realisation of the 'inferiority of others' from which he naturally develops 'a distinct superiority complex' and asserts: (FC)

'Destiny predisposed him to overcome the defects of his family, his caste, his race. And not only the defects, but the merits as well. He foresaw that he would someday reach this form of supreme freedom. He was already modelling himself on the image of the Hard and Solitary Man, the Man of Diamond, a fusion of Achilles and Orlando, the walking Man of Stone.' pp39-40

SCIASCIA
Leonardo

To Each His Own [A Ciascuno il Suo]
The Wine-Dark Sea [Il Mare Colore del Vino]

On the map Sicily lies like a football at Italy's boot waiting for kickoff; many Northern Italians would like to see it booted over the sidelines, away from their prestigious national team. If Italy for the foreigner conjures up images of Florence, Dante, Michelangelo, in short the prosperous North, Sicily is like an ugly pustule way down South throbbing with corruption, vendettas and a Hispanic code of honour that would be more at home in a Garcia Lorca play. But one Sicilian writer, Leonardo Sciascia, has done much to unravel the Sicilian psyche and probe the pulses that lie beneath its mafia culture. His books are short in the manner of Sartre and Camus but with a certain journalistic quality.

Sicilian magistrate Paolo Borsellino, accused by Sciascia of 'shop-window' mafia hunting in 1987, confessed owing much of his knowledge of the mafia to Sciascia's books 'in a period in which nobody spoke about it'. Sciascia plucks away the leaves of the *cosca* (artichoke), an alliance of families under one god-father, to bare the Sicilian soul. He delves into a consciousness which throughout history has been shaped by foreign invaders: the Greeks, the Arabs, the Normans and the Spanish. Sicilians have never, in effect, governed themselves. The result, Gesualdo Bufalino commented was to leave Sicilians with a hotchpotch of extremes: Muslim 'fanatical exultation', Norman 'loyalty and stern conscience' and a strict code of honour tempered only by a Greek 'sensitivity to light and harmony'.

Sciascia finds his way through the Sicilian labyrinth by surreptitious means. He hijacks the popular genre of the detective novel to hook his readers but gives them something more profound. *To Each His Own* has all the classic ingredients: murder, intrigue, suspense, even a detective. It reads like Garcia Marquez's *Chronicle of a Death Foretold*, and has the same detached, matter-of-fact relation of events. The difference lies in Sciascia's omniscient narrator and the fact that the culprit of the crime is eventually revealed (although not brought to trial). The perpetrator and the motive become clear not only to the celibate university lecturer obsessed with solving the crime; it is apparent to the whole community. But out of fear, cynicism, and lack of faith in the judiciary system, everyone shrugs their shoulders and keeps quiet. Professor Laurana himself never has any intention of exposing the crime; his intellectual curiosity was merely piqued by having an engrossing human crossword puzzle at his disposal. This, Sciascia hints, is symptomatic of a much deeper malaise in Sicilian society and one in which everyone, by family ties, politics or friendship, is implicated.

'To be strangers in truth or in guilt, or in truth and guilt together, is a luxury one can allow oneself only when there is an ordered system,' writes Sciascia. In Sicilian society, a loose structure based around favours and reciprocity fills the political vacuum. It never occurs to Professor Laurana to go to the authorities with his discovery because 'centuries of contempt...had heaped on the law and all those who were its instruments a conviction, still unquenched...that the highest right and truest justice, if one really cares about it, if one is not prepared to entrust its execution to fate or to God, can come only from the barrels of a gun.' This violent form of summary justice, Sciascia adds, is underpinned and perpetuated by the Catholic Church's 'concept of vicarious payment', in which cloistered virgins assume the sins of hotheaded patriarchs. In Sicily this form of payment has become the 'agonising religion' of the family.

The Ransom (in the *Wine-Dark Sea* collection) concerns a marriage between two families of rival neighbouring towns: dull socialist Grotte and festive mafia stronghold Racalmuto (Sciascia's hometown). The bride's father (from Grotte) is obliged to make a deal with the Procurator General of Palermo to ensure his son-in-law is not brought to trial for the callous killing of a peasant. The bribe or 'ransom' he must pay is to

give his youngest daughter's hand in marriage to the Procurator General of Palermo, a sacrifice she accepts unquestioningly. However it also signifies the ransoming of hostile Racalmuto by Grotte and is a metaphor for the complicated relationships in which Sicilians are locked by fate. *Euphrosyne*, a medieval tale of murder and honour, also explores these complicated binds based on passions, intrigues and circumstances.

If the core of Sicilian life is the family, which rests on a staunch sense of pride and protection of its honour, then the broader 'family' is the mafia. *A Mafia Western* (again in *The Wine-Dark Sea*) deals with an odd occurrence that breaks the usual pattern of violence among rival mafia factions. Sciascia describes this pattern as one in which the younger and older members vie for power. Usually, the violence intensifies until the two sides agree to sit down and negotiate. Indeed, excessive brutality on one side usually indicates its desire for peace. However, on this particular occasion the violence continues unabated, fueled by a young man's wrath against the mafia for preventing him from marrying the girl of his choice. He eventually receives his come-uppance at the hands of the 'family', which seeks to restore the old order, though not before wreaking havoc. Once again, Sciascia highlights Sicilian reluctance to seek help from the law, as a young mother covers up the murder of her son (who has been killed by the man he was trying to murder). The reader senses her full awareness of the circumstances of his death, which are made to seem even more appalling by the stoical manner in which she accepts it.

Catholic and religious imagery permeate Sciascia's writing, giving it an exuberant and sensual quality. He is quintessentially Sicilian, writing about Sicilian feelings and tied to his characters by the same network of affinities and sensibilities. We are told that the train announcer in *The Wine-Dark Sea* evokes for the passengers 'a vision of the face of a woman just past the first flush of youth floating in the evening sky among the overhead lines of the Termini station'. Signora Luisa's tight-fitting black dress in *To Each His Own* brings to Professor Laurana's mind the 'abundant languid nudity of a Delacroix odalisque'. But passion, jealousy and intrigue are related with a laconic detachment reminiscent of many Latin American authors. Laurana's erotic fixation with Signora Luisa is brought to an abrupt halt with the bland statement 'And thus passed the whole month of October.'

Sciascia brings to his stories a wonderful Mediterranean lightness and humour. The story *The Land Crossing* is a wry tale of Sicilian emigrés to the United States duped by an unscrupulous sea captain. They sail for twelve days full of illusions and grand ideas about their new homeland. But when they come ashore they are astonished by how similar the roads look until their feeble attempts at English are greeted by a torrent of verbal abuse in their own Sicilian dialect. In *Demotion* a comic analogy is drawn between the demotion of a local saint and the removal of Stalin from the mausoleum. *A Matter of Conscience* shows the disquiet a confession of infidelity in a woman's magazine sows amongst a bunch of men at a social club. In these stories Sciascia affectionately jibes at the flaws and idiosyncrasies of Sicilian life in a way that avoids being patronising, perhaps because Sciascia himself belongs to this world.

The 'wine-dark sea' in the story of the same name is the red-streaked sea separating Sicily from Italy. It sums up the passionate nature of Sicily, its power to intoxicate. A Northern Italian engineer travels by train from Rome to Sicily in the company of a lively Sicilian family of schoolteachers, their two unruly sons and a quiet meditative girl we know is a relative. The train journey itself mirrors the reader's journey through Sciascia's personal Sicilian landscape, and here, too, Sciascia's affection for his characters shines through. Bianchi and his family evolve from colourless strangers to complex people with their own view of the world as they grow lively and excitable, the children more and more undisciplined. They are never simple; they glow as individuals more, Sciascia suggests, than their Northern counterparts, both Italian and European. Nene is undisciplined because in Sicily there are no rules other than the 'bonds of affection'; but he is also quick-witted and generous. Societies that view children as a problem, says Bianchi (Sciascia's mouthpiece in the story), have a problem of continuity: in order to put satellites in space you must believe in future generations.

Reading Sciascia one has the impression that one is already walking the streets of a small Sicilian town, listening to the noises of the streets and feeling the murmurs of past love affairs and murders issuing up from the earth to mingle with the present. HB

The Day of the Owl [Il Giorno della Civetta]

'Mafia' is an Arab word that means 'hidden place' or 'meeting in a hidden place'. In Sicily it is used to denote 'a criminal association with the aim of illegally enriching its members...that places itself as an intermediary between private property and labour; a parasitical intermediary of course, acting through the use of violence.'

That is how the Sicilian writer Leonardo Sciascia defines the Mafia and in this novel he produces a 'fictional illustration' of its nature. Against the background of an inert island village two ways of thinking, two apparently irreconcilable Italys confront each other: that of the local Mafia thug which declares itself through murder, and the Northern way of the *carabiniere* captain Bellodi, a former partisan and a convinced democrat. Given the task of investigating the fatal shooting of Salvatore Colasbena, the captain tries to take the chain of responsibility right up to the local mafia boss, Mariano Arena, and to arrest him as the originator of the crime. During his interrogation of Arena the captain's loyalty to the state and its laws square up against the distorted logic of the *mafioso* and the veil is lifted from a criminal phenomenon that has its origins in Sicilian history. Political forces protect Arena from all accusations but in the end this doesn't break the moral resistance of the captain, who is left with a clearer and more sensitive vision of Sicilian problems.

Presented as a detective story, the book gets its power from the important question: Why is there a Mafia? Why does a man become a *mafioso*? From within contemporary Sicily itself, afflicted by what seems to be an inescapable curse, comes the voice of an urbane and responsible writer. FC

'Bellodi told the story of a medical officer in a Sicilian prison who took it into his head, quite rightly, to remove from the mafia convicts the privilege of residing permanently in the prison hospital. The prison was full of genuine sick cases, even some tubercular ones, living in cells and common dormitories, while these mafia chiefs, bursting with health, occupied the sick-bay in order to enjoy better treatment. The doctor gave orders for them to be sent back to their ordinary quarters and for the sick to be admitted to the hospital. The doctor's instructions were disregarded by both warders and governor. The doctor wrote to the Ministry. The next thing that happened was that one night he was summoned to the prison where, he was told, a prisoner had urgent need of him. He went. At one point in the prison he suddenly found himself alone among the convicts; and he was then beaten up with skill and precision by the mafia chiefs. The warders noticed nothing.' p119

One Way or Another [Todo Modo]

While meditatively travelling around the countryside, a painter happens upon the Zafer hermitage, a sort of inn for spiritual retreats. These are led by Don Gaetano, a cultivated and intellectual priest who, along with the artist, is the chief figure in this story. The artist, curious about the place, decides to stay there for a few days. His stay coincides with the arrival of a group of politicians gathered for a session of spiritual exercises and he becomes a witness to what ought to be a period of self-recollection, a turning away from the mundane world towards God and oneself, but actually turns into a grim scenario in which a series of murders takes place.

These happenings deeply shake the order, bringing into their peaceful haven the dynamics of the wider world, of political power and money, which attracts diverse observations and comments from both priest and painter. Thus two distinct psychological dimensions, the creative and the religious, confront each other in debate in the presence of a political world which emerges here as having no spiritual dimension at all, being occupied with empty, instant gratification.

Sciascia focuses on an area which Italian literature has avoided: the confrontation between the secular intellectual and Christianity. Don Gaetano's words prophetically warn against the mingling of the Church and political power while the artist admits to an existential and ideological unease which finds no answers. Altogether the book, read in the light of the present moral and political ruin of Italy through corruption, rings out as an alarming prediction, a case of literary clairvoyance that makes the novel seem as if written precisely for today. FC

"'You — excuse me — you have no idea what these church-and-hearth people are capable of, these people with their missals in hand who say they love their neighbour as themselves... In just two months — and I can't wait to see the day — I will have completed thirty years of service with the police. Well, the most ferocious crimes I've come across — the most rationally planned and best camouflaged, and also the maddest and most easily detectable — have been committed by men and women whose knees were swollen like this" — his hand modelled a plump, rounded loaf — "from kneeling at altar rails and confessional gratings... Some, of course, were sex crimes. But the greatest part, believe me, were committed for money. And most always for money to be inherited from someone's nearest and dearest.'" pp104-105

The Moro Affair [L'Affaire Moro]

Written shortly after the events it tells of, this book reconstructs the kidnapping of Aldo Moro, president of the Christian Democratic Party, by the Red Brigades in 1978. At that time Moro was successfully promoting the idea of communist participation in the government as a way of moving Italy out of political deadlock and stagnation.

Sciascia's version of events points to a rather murky scenario in which 'reasons of state' rather than humane considerations informed the government's actions. Instead of giving a blow-by-blow account Sciascia dwells on the cowardly conduct of the politicians who refused to negotiate with the terrorists — thereby condemning an innocent man to death. He bases these observations on Moro's letters from captivity to his friends and party colleagues, which attempted to persuade them to take a position more favourable to negotiation, one that might have saved his life.

Sciascia shows that the Christian Democrats denied Moro the respect due to a man who was one of their most important leaders, dismissing the letters as the dubious result of coercion and thereby sanctioning his death. This book is an act of accusation, opposing itself to the treacherous reasoning that placed political convenience above the life of a man. FC

'It's as if a dying man had risen from his bed, leapt into the air to swing from the chandelier like Tarzan from the liana, then rushed to the window and vaulted out to land, hale and hearty, in the street. The Italian State has revived. The Italian State is alive and strong , safe and sound. For a century it has consorted with the Sicilian Mafia, the Neapolitan Camorra, the Sardinian bandits. For three decades it has exploited corruption and incompetence, wasted public funds in streams and rivulets of unpunished embezzlement and fraud. For ten years it has quietly accepted what de Gaulle, while putting an end to it, called 'recreation' — schools occupied and vandalized and acts of juvenile violence against comrades and teachers alike. But now, confronted with Moro's sequestration by the Red Brigades, the Italian State rises up strong and impressive. Who dares question its strength, its impressiveness? No one. And least of all Moro in the 'People's Prison'.

Nenni had said: 'The Italian State is strong with the weak and weak with the strong'. Who are the weak today? Moro, his wife and children, those who think the State should have been and must be strong with the strong.'

Candido: Or, a Dream dreamed in Italy [Candido]

Written against our own heavy-spirited times, this novel is a free adaptation of Voltaire's *Candide*. It's the story of Candido Munafò, born in Sicily in 1943, when the advancing Allies' gunfire could already be heard. Candido's mother runs off with an American, then his father kills himself and he is entrusted to the care of a tutor, the Rural Dean Lepanto, a heretic by vocation, who gives him an education rather modern in spirit. Candido follows in his teacher's footsteps, experiencing the same disillusionment and alienation from two of the great faiths of our age: Catholicism and Communism.

Candido's desire for freedom, his belief in himself and the values of his childhood make him part company with Communism, a philosophy that he at one time embraces, in the same way as authentic Christian values push Lepanto to abandon the cloth. Their respective *crises de conscience* eventually ensure their freedom but only Candido, 'child of fortune and happy', achieves a real spirituality, through a relationship with life that allows him to benefit from it in every way.

All in all a brilliant fable in which irony and narrative inventiveness pave the way for the critique of a stagnant society enervated by ideologies and corrupted by false myths, a society from which only the spirit of liberty and passion for life can save one. Candido has both of these, a 'love for life like a strong tenacious root'. FC

'They stayed together talking until it was evening, until in the now dark room they were separated not only by the table but also by shadows; yet not exactly separated, for their voices had acquired a different afflatus, their talk a new brotherliness. Wealth, poverty... Evil, good... Possessing power, possessing none... The fascism within us, the fascism without... "Everything that we want to combat outside ourselves," the Archpriest said, "is inside us, and we must first look for it and fight it inside ourselves... I believe that men who know themselves somewhat, who live and are conscious of living, are divided into two big categories: there are those who know that wealth is dead but beautiful and those who know that wealth is beautiful but dead... For me, wealth is still beautiful but more and more dead, more and more death."' pp45-46

Sicilian Uncles [Gli Zii di Sicilia]

Sicilian Uncles is the title given to four early stories that mark Sciascia's entry into real narrative writing, his journey from the realism of his first book *Le Parrochie di Regalpetra (The Parishes of Regalpetra)*, which was based on news items and historical events, to fiction. The stories' common background is Sicily, seen through the changes that history has imposed on the island. *The American Aunt* is about the experience of emigration while in *Stalin's Death* it's the belief in Communism as secular salvation that takes centre stage. Rather different and set in a previous epoch is *The Forty-Eighter*, in which Garibaldi's campaign and some of its consequences for Sicily are described, while *Antimony* recounts the dramatic story of a Sicilian miner who is a volunteer with the fascist legionaries fighting for Franco in the Spanish Civil War.

In all the stories one can see Sciascia's attempt to bring the 'natural' narrative material of Sicilian reality together with broader themes emerging from the needs of storytelling itself, to free the potential of local material from sterility by showing it in the light of wider events. FC

'The Americans were already in Regalpetra, when it became known that Mussolini had been arrested in Rome. The news seemed to come from another world, as already, for the previous fourteen days in Regalpetra, people had been giving vent to their feelings against every kind of Fascism with chisels, fire and spittle. Calogero felt a little sad, seeing Federation spies and local Fascist leaders in frenetic anti-Fascist zeal, going round with the Americans, whispering denunciations; to satisfy them, the Americans took away the political secretary, the mayor and the carabinieri marshal. Calogero judged the Americans to be *di prima informativa*, people who thought the first comer was right. The Russians would have reacted differently. To round off his indignation, the carabinieri sergeant came to tell him that the Americans didn't like the meetings he held in his shop. The Americans perhaps knew nothing about the meetings, but they certainly didn't please some of their go-betweens.

In an indulgent moment, Calogero cut two portraits of Stalin out of an American magazine, and put them in handsome frames, hanging one up in the workshop and the other in the bedroom, next to the Madonna of Pompei, which his wife had on her side of the bed. "Oh, that's your father is it?" she commented, bitterly, but seeing him turn ugly she said nothing more.' p67

Bread and Wine [Vino e Pane]

'Watch Silone,' said Camus. 'He's closely connected to his own landscape and yet wholly European.' *Bread and Wine*, the second novel that Silone wrote during his years in exile (from 1935 to 1936) is the book that established his reputation as a writer by demonstrating the breadth and depth of his vision.

The main character, Piero Spina, is a kind of revolutionary the like of which has never been seen before or since in contemporary literature. The essential difference between him and other rebels of his period, like those created by Malraux or Hemingway, is that the latter are usually depicted carrying out deeds of courage while Piero, through the presence of informers and because of an illness, is forced into inactivity. His revolt, subsequently, is more an inner than an outer one, but there is no doubt whatsoever about his moral irreconciliability with tyranny.

Within the revolutionary movement itself *Bread and Wine* was a courageous act of self-criticism, but it should be added that it was the strategy of the movement rather than its values that were under discussion. Written 'shortly after the fascist occupation of Abyssinia and during the Moscow Show Trials organised by Stalin to destroy the last remnants of opposition', as Silone points out, it was a book that early on prefigured the ideological crisis of our times that drags all political parties in its wake, old élites as much as new apparatchniks. FC

'As the time for the declaration of war on the radio approached the crowd in the streets grew thicker. Motorcycles, cars, bicycles, cars, trucks loaded with party and corporation officials arrived from everywhere. Donkeys, carts, bicycles and trucks arrived bringing cafoni (yokels — *Babel Guide*) from the valleys. Two brass bands marched through the streets, playing the same anthem over and over again ad nauseam. The bandsmen's uniforms were like those of animal tamers at the circus or porters at grand hotels, with magnificent gold braid and double rows of metal buttons on their chests. Outside a barber's shop there was a big placard showing some Abyssinian women with breasts dangling almost to their knees. A dense group of youths had formed in front of it, gazing at it goggle-eyed and laughing.' pp187-188

SOLDATI
Mario

The American Bride [La Sposa Americana]

This is a story about a man and two women: Edoardo, a lecturer in Italian who works in the United States, his wife Edith and her friend Anna, for whom Edoardo also falls — a classic love triangle. If Edith represents the tenacity and wholeness of sacred love, of a meaningful relationship based on mutual affection, then Anna is the irresistible siren of profane love, of inescapable carnality. The plot unravels along a trail of suspicions, lies and mutual psychological contortions against the backdrop of America, a country for which Soldati has a deep regard. For him the American Dream is very real, understood as two great constituent parts, freedom and space.

Soldati's clarity and agility as a writer rescue the novel from being predictable. It has a style that Pasolini praised as 'Lightness incarnate', a lack of authorial overbearingness that induces a magically fraternal relationship with the reader. FC

'Edith's hands were, perhaps, the part of her I had remembered with the most searing desire in those eleven long months of separation and waiting. They were fraternal hands, loyal, hard-working. Like a living symbol of the one woman who could be my companion for ever.' pp69-70

SVEVO
Italo

As a Man Grows Older/Senilità

Considered by some critics to be Svevo's masterpiece, more consummate and balanced than *The Confessions of Zeno*, this novel had no success when first published, passing completely unnoticed. Set in the author's beloved home city of Trieste, it tells the story of a provincial man, Emilio Brentani, who, like Alfonso Nitti in Svevo's *A Life*, harbours literary ambitions, and of his ill-fated love for the modest and ambivalent Angiolina. Intended by Emilio to be an understanding free of sentimental impedimenta, their relationship transforms itself instead into the most tormented of passions against whose force all his ambitions are dashed. The confirmation of Emilio's failure and ineptitude gradually forces him into ever greater compromises, exposing him to an uneven contest with his self-possessed and brilliant friend Balli, a sculptor. His plight also disrupts the life of his sister Amalia, one of the more admirable female characters in Svevo's works, and condemns him to eternal unhappiness, parted from Angiolina.

As in other novels by Svevo, the trap waiting to ensnare the protagonist is the gap between reality and fantasy, between the concreteness of facts and the ability to understand and participate in them. Emilio Brentani symbolises the convergence of irreconcilable tensions and his life mirrors the widespread inability to span the breach that has opened between the individual and the world that surrounds him. FC

'"I can kiss you without making any noise," he declared, and he pressed his lips against hers and held her mouth a prisoner, while she continued to protest; so that his kiss was broken into a thousand fragments, couched deliciously on her warm breath.' p28

The Confessions of Zeno [Conscienza di Zeno]

Zeno Cosini is an elderly businessman who turns to the new science of psychoanalysis to try to rid himself of a series of physical and mental ailments. His analyst makes him delve into his memory and write down his impressions of his past. Zeno accordingly begins the disjointed narration of the salient chapters of his life — his marriage, his father's death, his business — and from this we see a pattern of perpetual failure emerging, the portrait of an inept man continually overtaken by events. His neurosis has influenced every moment of his life, denying him any ability to make decisions, turning him into an idle dreamer, a melancholic and mocking spectator of events, equipped with an ever-ready sense of irony. Zeno's adversities lie at the heart of twentieth-century man's crisis of values, his struggle for identity, and they leave their stamp on him as a total existential failure.

Written after a 25-year silence, *The Confessions* is the last of Svevo's novels and certainly the richest in autobiographical themes. Zeno's irony illuminates the writer's detachment from reality, a detachment exacerbated by the lack of recognition afforded Svevo, who only found fame towards the end of his life and then mainly abroad. The Italian public and critics honoured him only rather belatedly. FC

'My father, like so many family men, was an adept in the art of least resistance. He was at peace with his family and with himself. He only read safe and moral books, not out of hypocrisy but from genuine conviction. I think he really believed in those sermons, and that it quieted his conscience to feel himself sincerely on the side of virtue. Now that I am getting old and beginning to approach the patriarchal state, I too feel that it is worse to preach immorality than to practise it. One may be driven to commit murder by love or hatred, but one can only advocate murder out of sheer wickedness.' p36

A Life [Una Vita]

Alfonso Nitti is a young man with a strong literary vocation who has come from the country to Trieste to work in a bank. Meeting Annetta, his employer's daughter, opens the doors of the sophisticated world to him and, sharing a passion for literature, they begin writing a four-handed novel together. When they fall in love with each other, he, dissatisfied and unhappy, detaches himself with the excuse of his mother's poor health. But he can't evade the crushing weight of reality he felt overwhelming him by running away: his mother's death and the news of Annetta finding a new love, throws him into the state of defeat and failure which is the trademark of Svevo's characters. He gives in to it and kills himself.

The book's title comes from Nitti's suicide; it's the end of a life, one of the many anonymous lives marked by tragic impotence, their natural impetus broken by rigid class conditioning.

Svevo's first novel is about ambition and innocence, about the desire for social improvement and faithfulness to one's own dreams. Svevo himself said of it many years later, in a letter to Valéry Larbaud; 'I read *A Life* again. James Joyce always said that a man has only one novel in him and when he writes others they are always versions of the same one. In this case my only novel would be *A Life*.'

'...she then gave him her definition of life. Life was when he kissed her; nothing else was worth a thing. She was expressly renouncing all else for his kiss, he thought. As he kissed her to show his gratitude, it occurred to him that she must despise him if she considered herself to have lost the right to all other happiness by giving herself to him.... Alfonso's happiness, if it existed, was diminished by a fear. Had this woman whose feelings and opinions had changed in a single hour maybe gone off her head? He felt himself reasoning as usual, calm, pulled along by his senses for short periods then satiated, and he could not imagine that in others emotion could always be maintained and equal intensity.' p169

Little Misunderstandings of No Importance [Piccoli Equivoci senza Importanza]

Vanishing Point [Filo d'Orrizonte, Donna di Porto Pim, Volatili del Beato Angelico]

Indian Nocturne [Notturno Indiano]

Antonio Tabucchi was born in Pisa in 1943. His first work of fiction appeared in 1975 and since then he has published over a dozen novels, collections of short stories and theatrical dialogues in a career that has made him one of the most representative of contemporary Italian writers. He is Professor of Portugese language and literature at the University of Genoa and recognised as the leading Italian scholar in this field. He is a specialist on the work of Fernando Pessoa, who he has translated into Italian. His most recent novel, Requiem, was published in 1992.

Tabucchi is a post-Kafkanian writer. His protagonists share with Kafka's a pervasive sense of anxiety and guilt. But there is a crucial difference: Kafka has bequeathed to us a world in which the mind is constrained, not just imprisoned but, as Milan Kundera has suggested, self-imprisoning, unable to think about anything other than the one obsessive topic: the trial, the surveyor's job...Tabucchi's characters, on the other hand, carry their horizon with them. That is the sense of the 'filo dell'orizzonte', the vanishing point, the horizon that is neither waiting to be crossed nor crowding in upon you, but always there at the same distance, always unreachable.

Tabucchi, moreover, is assailed by an anxiety that engenders a different hell from Kafka's, not the doubt as to how one's action will be judged but the uncertainty as to whether it matters, as to what matters and how it matters. This seems a peculiarly postmodern condition. It is a semiotic anxiety.

The world is full of signs and we do not know how to interpret them, even the ones we have put there ourselves. One could say that we suffer from 'a haunted imagination'. Things may appear to have more meaning than they really do; the seagull that appears on two 'significant' occasions in Vanishing Point may be such a case. Other things we may choose not to give meaning to, either because the really have none or because they have so much that we cannot cope with it. Both types creep into the title of Little Misunderstandings of No Importance. 'Of no importance' here can mean two things: either that it really doesn't matter or that it matters so much that it's beyond repair, 'senza rimedio'. 'It really doesn't matter,' one says to the friend who has just smashed a priceless ornament — and perhaps, if the event is so cataclysmic that the world is changed as a result of it, it really doesn't matter, nothing matters anymore.

The question of how much weight to attribute to events and to their interpretations is the very condition of the haunted imagination. The haunted imagination's first preoccupation is a desire for something or someone else which, or who, will answer a need or a question. This search for an other invariably turns into a discovery, or partial discovery, of the self. This is a theme which Tabucchi foregrounds both in Indian Nocturne (in which an archivist unknowingly pursues his alter-ego across the sub-continent) and in Vanishing Point. The latter has more than a hint of the Sciascia school of detective fiction about it, beginning as a detective story of sorts, although what is mysterious is not the motive for the murder but the motive for the investigation. It gradually dawns on the investigator, Spino, (some time after it has dawned on the reader) that in trying to find out about the anonymous victim he is trying to discover something about himself. And characteristically, he articulates this point by addressing it to another, the doctor-turned-jazz-pianist Harpo:

'Who are you to yourself? Do you realise that if you wanted to find that out one day you'd have to look for yourself all over the place, reconstruct yourself, rummage in old drawers, get hold of evidence from other people, clues scattered here and there and lost? You'd be completely in the dark you'd have to feel your way.'

The search represented by the pseudo-detective story of Vanishing Point takes another form in Woman of Porto Pim, a sort of travel book about the Azores. Near the beginning the author summarises the strange experience of some English travellers in the 1840s:

'The houses, however, seemed to have bizarre shapes. When they got to the village they realised why. The fronts of all the houses had been made with the prows of sailing ships; they had a triangular floor plan, some were made with good hard woods, and the only stone wall was the one that closed the three sides of the triangle. Some of the houses were quite beautiful, the amazed Englishman tells us, their interiors scarcely looking like houses at all since almost all the furnishings — lanterns, seats, tables and even beds — had been taken from the sea. Many had portholes for windows and since they looked out over the precipice and the sea below they gave the impression of being in a sailing ship which has landed on top of a mountain.' p110

These houses 'made of the sea' are like a figure of the book itself. The archipelago is represented by a variety of means: the memory of the narrator and the inhabitants, stories, legends, documents, biography, a map, historical description, dreams and a bibliography of earlier writers' impressions, those 'honest travel books' whose value Tabucchi extols in his prologue. From none of these can the reader derive any composite picture of the Azores, and what is interesting about this and The Flying Creatures of Fra Angelico is Tabucchi's refusal to pull the fragments together (as Calvino, for example, might have tried to do with some linking device, however rudimentary)

The haunted imagination's second preoccupation is with what we have done and where it is taking us, our collective past and future, what we may call 'history'. The anxieties of history are particularly evident in Tabucchi's most recent collection of stories, L'Angelo Nero (The Black Angel), so far published only in Italian. In these black stories, Tabucchi's characteristic world-weariness gives way to a more bitter despair, as the collapse of the older generation's rationalist culture allows something that has ben repressed to emerge. With themes that include the behaviour of colonial troops in Angola, Céline and the new Right and the 1943-45 Italian civil war seen from the perspective of the fascist Republic of Salò, Tabucchi contemplates the horror of a history which will not go away and which triumphantly resists the efforts of enlightened culture to move beyond it.

The third preoccupation of the haunted imagination has to do with this anxiety over history as well, because it highlights the insistence of the Unconscious in our culture. There is a chilling phrase near the beginning of Vanishing Point:

'...he knows that Sara dreams of their impossible departure. He knows because it isn't difficult to get close to her dreams.'

It's not unusual for an artist to try to get in touch with the creative imagination of another artist. Tabucchi has done it with Fra Angelico, as Elsa Morante had done twenty years before. He has gone further, and in Sogni di Sogni (Dream of Dreams) imagines the dreams of artists whom he admires. There is, however, something disturbing in the realisation that in Tabucchi the imagination is not a private world, nor is it entirely innocent. The way that people get close to other people's dreams in Vanishing Point is through an intermediate body of images, which in that novel is the cinema, but which could be any other language or system of images. The essential point is that it does not belong to us individually but does very considerably determine how we imagine.

Haunted by the search for the other, haunted by the memories of history, haunted by its own promiscuity, the imagination in Tabucchi is the site of a troubled writing that captures well the anxieties of this fin de siècle. MC

TONDELLI
Pier Vittorio

Separate Rooms [Le Camere Separate]

This is the classic romantic journey of the alienated, solitary artist with a lust to travel life's uncomfortable borderlands. Tondelli, born 1955, made the journey in the 1970s and 80s so his reports are fresher than most. Here are bad acid trips to make you squirm, a disco so sweaty and loud you'll want to get out of there very quickly, in fact all the shock immediacy of very current writing, as in this image; 'a seaside town on the Adriatic coast...and the light is like the light in a studio set for a pop promo...'

Tondelli's work stands out too in its urgent and convincing honesty. He doesn't spare his own ego and although the gay essayist James Kirkup called Separate Rooms 'a beautifully written...homosexual Romeo and Juliet' Tondelli makes abundantly visible the destructiveness and self-indulgence in the loves of an intellectual with time on his hands. Without a doubt Tondelli worked at the level of honesty that differentiates real writing from the cosy substitute product. RL

'Every year autumn ushers in the same feelings. A need for silence and solitude and recollection. A need to sleep. To take stock. A need for introspection. The earth summons him unto her and invites him to gather his thoughts. And Leo, born in the glow of a late summer's day...hears this summons and follows it.' p43

VASSALLI
Sebastiano

The Chimera [La Chimera]

A historical novel which is very different from the tosh historical romances that clog the bookshops and public libraries of England and America. In fact the opposite of a 'romance' in its story of a beautiful, intelligent young girl executed by the religious bigots of the Counter-Reformation, after inadvertently getting caught up in the crossfire of rural and ecclesiastical realpolitik. This is a however a deeply enjoyable book that gives an unusual degree of insight into the superstitious rural world from which today's urban and secular Italy emerged.

Vassalli is a writer committed to connecting our rootless and distracted present to its history and confronting this particular period, the last pre-rationalist epoch in Europe, has a special importance today as thinking people everywhere have to deal with the rise of modern fundamentalisms, which generally possess, like the Holy Inquisition that tortured and burnt the heroine of The Chimera, a great thirst for meting out punishments to those who question their 'God-given' authority. RL

'The story of the Blessèd Panacea...is that of a luckless young shepherdess, born in 1368 in a village in the Novarese hill-country and dead at a tender age. The first misfortune in her life — a life beset with tragedies! — was very likely the name, Panacea, which her witless parents had imposed on her; but thereafter followed many others, each worse than the last. Orphaned on her mother's side — say the biographers, and so that day repeated Bishop Bascapè — she was slaughtered at fifteen years old by her stepmother, infuriated with her because she did nothing but pray. She had no sweetheart as did other girls of her age, she did not tend the flock, she did not spin the wool. She did nothing. She just prayed from morn till night and her stepmother beat her to death.' p164

VERGA
Giovanni

The House by the Medlar Tree [IMalavoglia]

First published in 1881, this bitter novel is the first part of a narrative cycle intended to foreground the life of the humble, the disinherited, the perennially defeated. The painful story of the Malavoglias, a fishing family, unwinds against the backdrop of a Sicilian village, Aci-Trezza. An honest, hardworking family who live under the authority of Old 'Ntoni, the Malavoglias are ruined by the ambitious yearnings of the grandson, Young 'Ntoni. A failed investment and the subsequent loss of their only material wealth — their boat Provvidenza — plunge them into a chain of mishaps, on top of which come debts they cannot honour. Their economic ruin unleashes a moral decline on the part of Young 'Ntoni, who refuses to bow to the fate that his namesake has always accepted. Incapable of joining in with the family's resigned passivity, the young man slides into a dissolute and idle lifestyle and after a wild binge ends up in prison, dragging everyone into dishonour with him. This seals the family's descent into the underworld. Only the youngest, Alessi, manages to climb out and rebuild his life.

Verga's pessimistic vision focuses on an existence ruled by the iron laws of seemingly inescapable poverty and a social oppressiveness that lends its burdensome tone to the whole novel. The world of the Malavoglias is a small one and its damnation lies in its relationship with the larger world that towers over it and suffocates it, represented by the higher social spheres; the law and the state. FC

'Padron Cipolla personally knew why it never rained now as it used to do. "It never rains nowadays because they've put up that dratted telegraph wire, which attracts all the rain and draws it away... it did this because there was a sort of juice inside the wire like the sap in a vine tendril, and in the same way it drew water from the clouds and carried it away, to where it was needed more... and that was why they had passed a law saying that anyone breaking a telegraph wire should go to prison."' p38

Mastro Don Gesualdo [Mastro Don Gesualdo]

The last fruit of Verga's artistic maturity and translated into English by D.H.Lawrence no less, this novel tells the story of a man who, from humble beginnings, through struggle and hard work and not without shrewdness and a certain lack of scruples, has accrued wealth, power and fertile land. The price he pays for his rise on the social scale is a hostility that surrounds him everywhere: misunderstood and unloved by his family, governed by cupidity, he lives a troubled and unhappy life, secretly longing for peace and affection. Consumed by evil, he suffers an inglorious decline not only of his physical strength but also of his hopes, which are dashed as, gravely ill, he witnesses the squandering of his fortune by the daughter he wished to have educated in the traditional manner of the nobility but who has married a bungling, greedy inadequate.

The parable of Mastro Don Gesualdo tells of another kind of defeat that here, unlike with 'Ntoni Malavoglia in Verga's The House by the Medlar Tree, befalls a man lacking in all idealism and moral judgement, who has sacrificed everything to possess material goods. In Don Gesualdo the author tries to focus on the corruption of a soul, the impossibility of a person born into poverty of bettering himself without losing too much — the impossibility of acquiring worldly goods without losing one's way in the process. FC

'It was precisely on the balcony of the alley, looking squinting on to the square, for the second-grade guests and the poor relations: Dame Clara Macrì, so humble and so shabby that she seemed like a servant; her daughter Mistress Agrippina, a house-nun , a girl with such a moustache, and a pimpled brown face like a begging friar, and two eyes black as sin which roved round among the men. In the first row Cousin Don Ferdinando, more inquisitive than a child, who had pushed himself forward with elbow-thrusts, and was stretching his neck out of his black cravat to look toward the Great Square, like a tortoise, with his grey, rolling eyes, his sooty, pointed chin, his long, quivering Trao nose, his queue curving in like the tail of a dog on his greasy collar that came up to his hairy ears; and his sister, Donna Bianca, poked away behind him, her shoulders rather bent, her breast thin and flat, her hair smooth, her face meagre and washed-out, dressed in flannelette in the midst of all her fine relatives.' p37

Run! [Il Tennis nel Bosco]

Viganò is a new voice in Italian literature and the stories here, particularly *Verklärte Nacht*, *Tennis Court* and *Fiat Panda* show an adventurousness and real freshness in the writing. Using a highly compressed, almost 'perverse' way of describing things and feelings Viganò has made some real breakthroughs in talking about an everyday world. In *Fiat Panda* for example, the banality of a car arriving along a deserted stretch of road is described in a curious, oblique way as; 'a car is coming along, its high speed reduced by the perspective'. Our experience of a car speeding down an empty road, its sound announcing it is suggested through perspective, so that the nuances of a real phenomenon are evoked by the psychologically real illusion we call 'perspective'.

The other originality of Viganò is her treatment of little explored themes and realities. The protagonist of *The Garage* is an overweight incestual delinquent and yet, without hiding her loathing for this character, he too gets a platform, an explanation of how he came to be that way, and so we are forced to look deeper into the cookpot of Italian family life and see what's stewing. One thing in there, according to confirmed feminist Viganò, is the notorious Italian *mammismo*, the idolatory of mother for son and the subsequent dependence it fosters. *The Garage* seems to take mammismo to a logical and horrible conclusion.

The originality of the story *Verklärte Nacht* on the other hand is more structural than thematic; its narrative form emulates the 'fractured continuity' of modern music — while it's hard to describe how Viganò achieves this, it is undoubtedly an exceptional and virtuoso piece of writing, like the Schoenberg concerto it is named for.

The stories in Run! depict what is quite an unfamilar Italy to most non-Italians; the contemporary world of ordinary city dwellers. The beauty of this collection is, apart from the writing, that it connects English-speaking readers with the real lives of Italians living familiar lives; so that for once it is possible to break through the veil of exoticism and stereotypes to encounter a similar, yet different human world. RL

'I wedge myself into an unexpected parking space created by a curved recess in the rubber barrier dividing off the bus lane, turn the key and switch off the motor. I check in my pocket for the concert ticket. With the other hand I grip the umbrella but a gentle lethargy overcomes me inside the warm car. The lights all around are already a performance, making their glittering escape in noisy spinning droplets, lengthening, then distorting into bubbles and then extinguishing themselves in streams of rain draining away. They gleam and ignite and the whole hypnotic rhythm beats out a metre that is consummated inside other rhythms, in a huge machinery overhanging everything else.' Verklärte Nacht

VITTORINI
Elio

The Red Carnation [Il Garofano Rosso]

The desire to be grown up, to move into adulthood with all its rites and rhythms is what inspires Alessio Mainardi, the main protagonist of this story about achieving political and human maturity in the early years of Fascism. Alessio's education sentimentale starts with Giovanna, the young girl who loves him and gives him the red carnation of the title, and is completed in the murky sensual relationship he has with Zobeida the prostitute — and all this against a background of political turmoil.

Vittorini himself criticised the book for its lack of unity and the disharmony between its various aims and stylistic approaches, calling it 'a book marked by the desire to avoid the vexatious burden of balance and deliberation'. In fact there are two tensions that rule the book: on the one hand the need to make it a work of realism, a document faithful to its times, and on the other the desire to maintain a creative control over reality so as to be able to transform it into fantastic and symbolic forms. FC

'I was sixteen years old, nearly seventeen; I already liked to play the grown-up and be with the real grown-ups, the lads of eighteen and older...to talk and smoke under the rust-coloured café awning.'

Conversation in Sicily [Conversazione in Sicilia]

This is the story of a journey the author imagines making in his native Sicily following a letter from his father announcing the abandonment of the family home. Vittorini's fictional double is Silvestro, a typographer who lives in Milan and suffers a disturbing, vague desire for action that has no real outlets and renders him incapable of getting to grips with anything. He reacts by setting off on a journey into his own past, not just to recover it (or, even worse, to relive it) but to find some promise in it, a reason to live in the present that would allow him to escape from his stalemated existence.

From Silvestro's meetings and conversations with various characters and above all with his mother emerges a portrait of an 'abused world', a dramatically awful situation permeated by poverty and sickness and weighed down by blind oppresion. Out of all this though comes an urgent need — which Vittorini feels too — for a new kind of consciousness.

This is Vittorini's masterpiece, a poetic and moral journey in search of a remedy for the Sicilian malaise and of a real alternative to the deceitfulness of today. FC

'That winter I was prey to vague indefinable longings. I can't say what they were, that's not the story I have to tell. I only need to say that they were vague, not heroic, not alive; longings anyway, for the lost human being.'

VOLPONI
Paolo

The Memorandum/Il Memoriale

Volponi's first novel, originally published in 1962, progresses along a double track: on one side the development of a medical case, on the other the experience of a worker in a 'neo-capitalist' factory. Albino Saluggia recounts how he gets a job in the factory at the end of the war after living through the experiences of emigration, serving in the army and finally prison. His strong desire for a new, different kind of life makes him enthusiastic about his job notwithstanding the tuberculosis that is undermining his body and his psychological frailty. For him the factory becomes his central

existential investment but it becomes an object of frustration as he discovers the inhumanity that underpins it. His sense of disappointment exacerbates his old psychological problems and the more the factory's welfare system tries to help him the more paranoid he becomes. As his state worsens the factory continues to look after him, keeping his job for him and accepting all his excesses up to the point where he commits the one act that can't be accepted by the management's logic — he goes on strike. That marks the end of everything and he gets the sack.

Replying to reviewers, the author said in an interview in 1962:

'*The Memorandum*...doesn't have any literary or ideological programme; it simply examines in a relentless, doggedly scientific way the reality of its main character, just because that is a partial, individual reality. The strength of its analyses aren't just polemical but necessary and positive . and the work's scientific nature allows it to come to general conclusions.'

CONTRIBUTORS

Ray Lombardo (Ray Keenoy BA Hons)
works as a literary translator from Italian and is founding editor
of the Babel Guides series.
Fiorenza Conte Dott.Lett.
lives in Siena and works freelance for various publishers
Helen Blücher-Altona MA
works in publishing and is currently collaborating on the
Babel Guide to Latin American Fiction in Translation
Michael Caesar MA
is Professor of Italian Literature at the University of
Birmingham
Patrick Curry PhD
writes on various topics, currently contributing to a book on
Postmodernism
Lola Rinvolucri BA
formerly of the BBC, now a freelance writer
Michèle Roberts
is a well-known writer and critic. Her
review originally appeared in New Statesman and Society;
to whom thanks.
All other reviews in this guide were
specially written for the Babel Guide

Illustrator
Jackie Wrout

Petrignani, Sandra
Pirandello, Luigi
Pitigrilli,
Pratolini, Vasco
Pressburger, Giorgio & Nicola
Samona, Carmelo
Savinio, Alberto
Sciascia, Leonardo
Silone, Ignazio
Soldati, Mario
Svevo, Italo
Tabucchi, Antonio
Tondelli, Pier Vittorio
Vassalli, Sebastiano
Verga, Giovanni
Viganò, Valeria
Vittorini, Elio
Volponi, Paolo

Database of Italian fiction translated in UK

This database is for anyone who wants to read Italian writers' work in English. Its main goal is to let you know what is available. The *reviews* section of the guide emphasizes books that are currently in print and that you can find or order at your bookshop now but this section includes *all* the contemporary (written after 1900) fiction we could trace.

Please note the price and availability of books changes from day to day as publishers withdraw, re-price and reprint. This database is a handy guide but for the latest information on a particular book ask your bookseller or librarian. Remember your bookseller can order you any in-print book and that public libraries can get you any current or out-of-print title, often at no charge.

Abbreviations:
HB = hard cover edition
PB = paperback edition
O/P = out of print (this means your bookshop can only sell you a copy if they have one in stock already. The publisher may reprint it though, so check later.)

ALERAMO
Sibilla
Woman, A
1979
Donna, Una
1906
VIRAGO
PB
183
O/P
Woman, A
1992
Donna, Una
1906
CALIFORNIA UP
HB
183
24

ALESSANDRIA
Pia D'
Bull's Eye
1962
Tiro al bersaglio
1958
Chanter, J R
H HAMILTON
128
O/P

ALEXANDER (ED.)
Alfred
Stories of Sicily
1975
Alexander, Alfred
ELEK BOOKS
208
O/P

AMICIS
Edmundo De
Cuore: The heart of a Boy
1986
Cuore
1889
Hartley, D
OWEN
14.95

ANTONIONI
Michelangelo
That Bowling Alley on the Tiber. Tales of a Director.
1986
Quel Bowling Sul Tevere
1983
OUP

PB
208
O/P

ARAD
Luciana D'
Love without grace
1963
Insaziati, Gli
1961
Green, Peter
MULLER; LONDON
223
O/P

ARBASINO
Alberto
Lost Boy, The
1964
Ragazzo Perduto, Il (L'Anonimo Sardo)
Wall, B
FABER
186
O/P

ARPINO
Giovanni
Crime of Honour, A
1963
Delitto d'onore, Un
1961
Rosenthal, R
WEIDENFELD
250
O/P

BACCHELLI
Riccardo
Devil at Long Bridge, The
1929
Diavolo al Ponteluno, Il
1927
Williams, Orlo
LONGMANS
346
O/P

Fire of Milan, The
1958
Incendio di Milano, L'
1952
Nott, Kathleen
SECKER & WARBURG
302
O/P

Love Town
1930
Città degli Amante, La
1929
Williams, Orlo

DUCKWORTH
296
O/P

Mill on the Po, The
1952
Mulino del Po, Il
1938
Frenaye, F
HUTCHINSON
HB
591
O/P

Nothing New under the sun
1955
Mondo Vecchio Sempre Nuovo
1940
Hood, S
SECKER & WARBURG
518
O/P

Son of Stalin
1956
Figlio di Stalin
1953
Nott, K
SECKER & WARBURG
O/P

BALESTRINI
Nanni
Unseen, The
1989
Invisibili, Gli
1976
Heron, Liz
VERSO
HB
256
13.95

BANTI
Anna
Artemesia
1989
Artemesia
1953
Caracciolo, Shirley D.
NEBRASKA UP
HB
219
15.10

Artemesia
1995
Artemesia
1953
Caracciolo, Shirley D.
SERPENT'S TAIL
PB
219
8.99

BAROLINI
Antonio
Long Madness, A
1964
Pazzia Lunga, Una
Barolini, Helen
GOLLANCZ
308
O/P

BARTOLINI
Luigi
Bicycle Thieves
1952
Ladri di Biciclette
1948
Richards, C.J.
M.JOSEPH
O/P

BASSANI
Giorgio
Behind the door
1992 (1973)
Dietro la porta
1964
Weaver, W
QUARTET
PB
154
6.95

Garden of the Finzi-Continis
1978
Giardino dei Finzi-Continis
1965
Quigley, I
QUARTET
PB
6.95

Gold-Rimmed Spectacles, The
1960
Gli occhiali d'oro
1958
FABER
O/P

Heron, The
1993
Airone, L'

1968
Weaver, W
QUARTET
PB
192
7.95

Prospect of Ferrara, A
1962
Cinque Storie Ferraresi
1956
FABER
O/P

Smell of Hay, The
1975
*Odore di Fieno, L'(1972) &
Occhiali d'Oro(1958)*
1958
WEIDENFELD
193
O/P

Smell of Hay, The
1994
*Odore di Fieno, L'(1972) &
Occhiali d'Oro(1958)*
1958
Weaver, W
WEIDENFELD
PB
208
7.00

BENNI
Stefano
Terra!
1986
Terra!
Cancogni, A
PLUTO P
HB
12.50

Zoomers: Very Short Stories
1991
CLOCKTOWER P, SOUTH QUEENSFERRY
20
O/P

BERTO
Giuseppe
Anonymous Venetian
1973
Anonimo Veneziano
1971
Southorn, Valerie
HODDER
PB
78
O/P

Antonio in love
1969
Cosa buffa, La
1966
Weaver, W
HODDER
303
O/P

Brigand, The
1951
Brigante, Il
1951
Davidson, A.
SECKER & WARBURG
224
O/P

Incubus
1966
Male oscuro, Il
1964
Weaver, W
HODDER
O/P

Incubus
1969
Male oscuro, Il
1964
Weaver, W
PENGUIN
PB
O/P

Sky is Red, The
1972 (1948)
Cielo è rosso, Il
1946
Davidson, A
SHIRE PUBS: AYLESBURY
380
O/P

Sky is Red, The
1990
Cielo è rosso, Il
1946
Davidson, A
GREENWOOD P
HB
60.75

BEVILACQUA
Alberto
Califfa
1969
Califfa, La
1964
Fergusson II, Harvey
ALLEN & UNWIN
O/P

BIANCHI
Oliviero Honoré
Devil's Night
1961
Notte del diavolo
1957
Quigley, I
EYRE & S
188
O/P

BIANCIARDI
Luciano
La vita agra or It's a hard life
1965
Vita Agra, La
1962
Mosbacher, E
HODDER
191
O/P

BIASION, TOBINO & RIGONI-STERN
Renzo, Mario & Mario
Lost Legions, The. Three Italian War Novels.
1967
Colquhoun, A. & Cowan, Antonia
MACGIBBON & KEE: LONDON
O/P

BIGIARETTI
Libero
Convention, The
1965
Congreso, Il
1963
Gren, Joseph
MACMILLAN
179
O/P

BOITO
Camilo
Senso & Other Stories
1993
Senso ed altre storielle vane
1961
Donougher, C. & Conway, R.
DEDALUS, SAWTRY
PB
207
6.99

BOMPIANI
Ginevra
Old Heaven, New Earth
1996
Incantato, L' & Vecchio Cielo, Nuova Terra
1987, 1988
Lombardo, Ray & Wrout, Jackie
BOULEVARD: DIST. BY CENTRAL BOOKS
PB
6.95

BONA
Gian Piero
Naked Soldier, The
1963
Soldato Nudo, Il
1961
Benzimra, Lyon
BLOND
181
O/P

BONO
Elena
Widow of Pilate, The
1958
Morte d'Adamo
Kean, V
H HAMILTON
252
O/P

BORGESE, Ed.
Giuseppe Antonio
Italian Short Stories of To-day.
1946
May, E.I. & Treves, Piero
HARRAP
O/P
Rubé
1923
1921
Goldberg, Isaac
JOHN LANE
394
O/P

BRANCATI
Vitaliano
Antonio the great lover
1952
Bell'Antonio
1950
Kean, Vladimir
DOBSON
HB

O/P
Bell'Antonio
1993
Bell'Antonio
1950
Creagh, P
HARVILL
PB
320
8.99
Bell'Antonio
1993
Bell'Antonio
1950
Creagh, P
HARVILL
HB
320
14.99
Lost Years, The
1993
Anni Perduti
1941
Creagh, P
HARVILL
PB
207
7.99
Lost Years, The
1991
Anni Perduti
1941
Creagh, P
HARVILL
HB
207
13.99

BRELICH
Mario
Work of Betrayal
1991
Opera del Tradimento
1975
Rosenthal, R
MARLBORO PRESS
PB
238
8.50
Navigation of the Flood
1995
Shepley, J
MARLBORO PRESS
PB
114
7.95

BUFALINO
Gesualdo
Blind Argus
1989
Argo Il Cieco
1984
Creagh, P
HARVILL
HB
176
11.50

Blind Argus
1989
Argo Il Cieco
1984
Creagh, P
HARVILL
PB
176
7.99

Keeper of Ruins, The
1994
Uomo invaso, L'
1986
Creagh, P
HARVILL
HB
160
14.99

Keeper of Ruins, The
1994
Uomo invaso, L'
1986
Creagh, P
HARVILL
PB
160
8.99

Night's Lies
1990
Menzogne della Notte, Le
1988
Creagh, P
COLLINS
HB
158
O/P

Night's Lies
1991
Menzogne della Notte, Le
1988
Creagh, P
HARVILL
PB
158
7.99

Plague-sower
1988

Diceria dell'Untore
1981
Sartarelli, S
ERIDANOS P
HB
192
14.95

Plague-sower
1988
Diceria dell'untore
1981
Sartarelli, S
ERIDANOS P
PB
192
7.95

BUONO
Oreste Del
One Single Minute
1963
Intero Minuto, Un
1959
Lane, Helen R
FABER
215
O/P

BUSI
Aldo
Seminar on Youth
1988
Seminario sulla Gioventù
1984
Hood, S
CARCANET
HB
288
14.95

Seminar on Youth
1989
Seminario sulla Gioventù
1984
Hood, S
FABER
PB
288
6.99

Sodomies in Eleven Point
1992
Sodomie in Corpo ll
1992
Hood, S
FABER
PB
335
7.99

Sodomies in Eleven Point
1992

Sodomie in Corpo ll
1992
Hood, S
FABER
HB
343
O/P

Standard Life of A Temporary Pantyhose Salesman
1989
Vita standard di un venditore provvisorio di collant
1985
Rosenthal, R
FABER
HB
430
O/P

Standard Life of A Temporary Pantyhose Salesman
1990
Vita standard di un venditore provvisorio di collant
1985
Rosenthal, R
FABER
PB
430
5.99

BUZZATI
Dino
Catastrophe: The Strange Stories of Dino Buzzati
1981
Landry, J & C. Jolly
CALDER
139
O/P

Larger than life
1962
Grande Ritrato, Il
1960
Reed, H.
SECKER & WARBURG
154
O/P

Love Affair, A
1987 (1965)
Amore, Un
1963
Joseph Green
CARCANET
HB
299

O/P

Restless Night
1987 (1984)
Notti Difficili
1971
Lawrence Venutti
CARCANET
HB
122
O/P

Restless Night
Notti Difficili
1971
Lawrence Venutti
CARCANET
PB
122
O/P

Siren, The
NORTH POINT, US
PB
O/P

Tartar Steppe
1990
Deserto dei Tartari
1948
Hood, S
PALADIN
PB
214
O/P

CACCIATORE
Vera
Swing, and two other stories, The
1959
Strachan, W.J.
EYRE & SPOTTISWOODE
197
O/P

CAESAR,
A. & M. Ed.S
Quality of Light, The
1993
Emery, Ed et al
SERPENT'S TAIL
PB
256
8.99

CAETANI
Marguerite
Anthology of New Italian Writing
1951
LEHMANN
477
O/P

CALASSO
Robert
Ruin of Kasch, The
1994
Rovina di Kasch, La
1983
Weaver W, Sartarelli, S
CARCANET
HB
385
19.95

Marriage of Cadmus and Harmony, The
1993
Nozze di Cadmo e Armonia, Le
1989
Parks, T
CAPE
HB
403
15.99

Marriage of Cadmus and Harmony, The
1994
Nozze di Cadmo e Armonia, Le
1989
Parks, T
VINTAGE
PB
403
5.99

Marriage of Cadmus and Harmony, The
1983
Nozze di Cadmo e Armonia, Le
1989
Parks, T
SECKER
HB
224
10.95

CALVINO
Italo
Adam, One Afternoon
1992
Ultimo viene il corvo & la formica argentina
1949

Coloquhon,A. & Wright, P
MINERVA
PB
189
4.99

Castle of Crossed Destinies
1977
Castello dei destini incrociati
1977
SECKER & WARBURG
HB
129
18.99

Castle of Crossed Destinies
1978
Castello dei destini incrociati
1977
PICADOR
PB
5.99

Cosmicomics
1982 (1968)
Cosmicomiche
1965
Weaver, W
ABACUS
153
O/P

Cosmicomics
1994
Cosmicomiche
1965
Weaver, W
PICADOR
PB
160
5.99

Difficult Loves
1993
Amori difficili
MINERVA
PB
256
5.99

Difficult Loves & Plunge into Real Estate
1983
Amori difficili
Weaver, W et al
SECKER & WARBURG
HB
O/P

database of Italian fiction translated in UK

If on a Winter's night a Traveller
1993
Se un notte d'inverno un viaggiatore
1979
Weaver, W
EVERYMAN
HB
254
7.99

If on a Winter's Night a Traveller
1993
Se un notte d'inverno un viaggiatore
1979
Weaver, W
MINERVA
PB
4.99

Invisible Cities
1992
Citta invisibili
1975
Weaver, W
MINERVA
PB
O/P

Italian Folk Tales
1982
Fiabe Italiane
1956
Martin, G.
PENGUIN
PB
12.99

Italian Folk Tales
1982
Fiabe Italiane
1956
Martin, G.
HARCOURT BRACE
HB
763
19.95

Marcovaldo
1983
Marcovaldo
1963
Weaver, W
SECKER & WARBURG
HB
121
O/P

Marcovaldo or the seasons in Italy
1985
Marcovaldo
1963
Weaver, W
PICADOR, PAN
PB
121
O/P

Marcovaldo or the seasons in Italy
1993
Marcovaldo
1963
Weaver, W
MINERVA
PB
121
5.99

Mr Palomar
1986
Palomar
1983
Weaver, W
PICADOR
PB
O/P

Mr Palomar
1986
Palomar
1983
Weaver, W
PICADOR
PB
4.99

Mr Palomar
1986
Palomar
1983
Weaver, W
SECKER & WARBURG
HB
10.95

Our Ancestors: The Cloven Viscount, Baron in the Trees etc
1980
Visconte dimezzate
1960
SECKER & WARBURG
HB
10.95

Our Ancestors: The Cloven Viscount, Baron in the Trees etc
1992
1960
MINERVA
PB

382
5.99

Path to the nest of spiders, The
1956
Sentiero dei nidi di ragno
1947
Colquhoun, A
COLLINS
O/P

Path to the nest of spiders, The
1993
Sentiero dei nidi di ragno
1947
Colquhoun
ECCO PRESS
6.45

Road to San Giovanni, The
1993
Strada di San Giovanni, La
1990
Parks, T
CAPE
HB
144
12.99

Road to San Giovanni, The
1993
Strada di San Giovanni, La
1990
Parks, T
VINTAGE
PB
160
5.99

Six Memos for the Next Millenium
1992
Lezioni americane, sei proposte per
Creagh, P
CAPE
PB
136
7.99

Time and the Hunter
1983
Ti Con Zero
1967
ABACUS
PB
O/P

Time and the Hunter
1983

Ti Con Zero
1967
PICADOR
PB
4.99

Under the Jaguar Sun
1992
Sotto il Sole Giaguaro
1986
Weaver, W
VINTAGE
PB
86
4.99

Under the Jaguar Sun
1992
Sotto il Sole Giaguaro
1986
Weaver, W
CAPE
HB
96
10.99

Watcher, The & Other Stories
Giornata di una Scrutatore, La
1963
Weaver, W et al
SECKER & WARBURG
HB
O/P

CALY
Maria
Dons, The
1973
Swinglehurst, Pamela
M JOSEPH
192
O/P

CAMON
Ferdinando
Fifth Estate
1994
Quinto Stato, Il
1970
Shepley, J
QUARTET
PB
163
6.95

Life Everlasting
1991
Vita Eterna, La
1972
Shepley, J
MARLBORO PRESS

PB
189
7.50

CAMPANILE
Pasquale Festa
For Love, Only Love
1986
Per amore, solo per amore
1984
Weaver, W
FUTURA
PB
176
O/P

CANCOGNI
Manlio
Month in Paris
1962
Parigina, Una
1960
Williams, M-T & D
HEINEMAN
267
O/P

CAPRIA
Raffaelle La
Mortal Wound, The
1964
Ferito a morte
1961
Waldman, Marguerite
COLLINS
191
O/P

CARDELLA
Lara
Good girls don't wear trousers
1993
Carcaci, Diana di
HAMISH HAMILTON
HB
118
O/P

CARLO
Andrea De
Cream Train, The
1987
Treno di Panna, Il
1981
Gatt, J
OLIVE P, LONDON
HB
184
9.95

Cream Train, The

1987
Treno di Panna, Il
1981
Gatt, John
OLIVE P, LONDON
PB
5.95

CARLO
Silvano
Striking without tears
1973
Come fare lo sciopero con amore
1971
Penet, Raymond
M JOSEPH
92
O/P

CARPI
Fabio
Abandoned Places, The
1964
Luoghi abbandonati, I
1962
Quigley, I
HODDER
126
O/P

CASSIERI
Giuseppe
Bald Man, The
1963
Cocuzza, Il
1960
Rosenthal, R
SECKER & WARBURG
243
O/P

CASSOLA
Carlo
Bebo's Girl
1962
Ragazza di Bebo, La
1960
Waldman, Marguerite
COLLINS
256
O/P

Portrait of Helena
1975
Monte Mario
1973
Roberts, Sebastian
CHATTO
208
O/P

database of Italian fiction translated in UK

Fausto and Anna
1960
Fausto ed Anna
1952
Quigley, I
COLLINS
318
O/P

CASTELLANETA
Carlo
This Gentle Companion
1970
Dolce Compagna, la
Robert, S.
CHATTO
PB
O/P

Journey with father
1962
Viaggio col padre
1958
Darwell, W C
MACDONALD
PB
191
O/P

Until the next enchant-ment
1970
Incantesimi, Gli
1968
Kay, G
CHATTO
PB
296
O/P

CAVAZZONI
Ermano
Voice of the Moon
1990
Poema dei Lunatici
1987
Emery, Ed
SERPENT'S TAIL
PB
288
8.99

CECCHERINI
Silvano
Transfer, The
1966
Traduzione, La
1939
Quigley, I
HARVILL
O/P

CELATI
Gianni
Appearances
1991
Quattro novelle sulle apparenze
1987
Hood, S
SERPENT'S TAIL
PB
126
8.99

Voices from the Plains
1989
Narratori delle Pianure
1985
Lumley, Robert
SERPENT'S TAIL
PB
158
8.99

CESPEDES
Alba De
Bambolona, LA
1969
Bambolona, La
1967
Quigley, I
M JOSEPH
272
O/P

Best of Husbands, The
1953
Cielo e la terra, Il
1950
Frenaye, F
HEINEMANN
HB
O/P

Between then and now
1959
Prima e dopo
1955
Quigley, I
CAPE
O/P

Remorse
1963
Rimorso
Weaver, W
GREENWOOD P
HB
397
53.95

Secret, The
1957
Quaderno Proibito

1952
Quigley, I
HARVILL
250
O/P

Until the next enchant-ment
1968
Incantesimi, Gli
Kay, George
CHATTO
206
O/P

CHIARI
Piero
Man of Parts, A
1968
Spartizione, La
1964
Martines, Julia
CRESSET P
180
O/P

CIALENTE
Faustia
Levantines, The
1961
Ballata Levantina
1963
Quigley, I
FABER
O/P

CIBOTTO
Gian Antonio
Scano Boa
1963
Scano Boa
1961
Grigson, Jane
HODDER
127
O/P

COCCIOLI
Carlo
Eye and the heart, The
1960
Fabrizio Lupo
1952
Frechtman, Bernard
HEINEMANN
406
O/P

COLIZZI
Giuseppe
Night has another voice, The

1963
Notte ha un'altra voce, La
1958
Benzimra, Lyon
ABELARD-SCHUMAN
(RAVEN BKS): LONDON
207
O/P

COLQUHOUN
(ED.)
**Italian Regional Tales of
the nineteenth Century**
1961
Wall, B. et al
OXFORD UP
268
O/P

COMENCINI
Christina
Missing Pages,The
1993
Pagine Strappate, Le
1992
Dowling, G
CHATTO
PB
268
9.99

COMPAGNONE
Luigi
Curse of Melaria, The
1956
Vacanza delle Donne, La
1954
SPEARMAN
PB
110
O/P

CONSOLO
Vincenzo
**Smile of the Unknown
Mariner**
1994
*Sorriso dell'ignoto
Marinaio, Il*
1976
Farrell, Joseph
CARCANET
HB
128
14.95

CORDELLI
Franco
Pinkerton
1990
Pinkerton

Waugh, T
QUARTET
HB
185
12.95

CRESCENZO
Luciano De
Dialogues, The
1991
Oi Dialogoi
Bardoni, A.
PICADOR
PB
160
O/P

Thus Spake Bellavista
1988
Così parlò Bellavista
1977
Bardoni, A.
PICADOR, PAN
PB
5.95

D'ANNUNZIO
Gabriele D'
**Nocturne & Five Tales of
Love And Death**
1994
Rosenthal, R
QUARTET
PB
264
6.95

Child of Pleasure
1990
Piacere, Il
1889
Harding, G
DEDALUS, SAWTRY
PB
311
7.99

Flame of Life, The
1990
Fuoco, Il
1900
DEDALUS, SAWTRY
PB
O/P

Flame, The
1991
Fuoco, Il
1900
Basnett, S
QUARTET
PB
309

8.95
**Nocturne & Five Tales of
Love And Death**
1988
Notturno etc.
Rosenthal, R
MARLBORO PRESS
PB
264
O/P

Triumph of Death
1990
Triunfo della Morte
1894
Harding, Georgina
DEDALUS, SAWTRY
PB
315
7.99

Victim, The
1991
Innocente, L'
1892
Harding, G
DEDALUS, SAWTRY
356
7.99

Virgins of the Rocks
1899
Hughes, A
HEINEMANN
247
O/P

DEL GIUDICE
Daniele Del
Lines of Light
1989
Atlante Occidentale
1985
McAfee, N. & Fontanella,
C
VIKING
HB
160
O/P

DELEDDA
Grazia
After the Divorce
1985
Dopo il divorzio
1902
Ashe, S
QUARTET
PB
192
4.95

database of Italian fiction translated in UK

Chiaroscuro and other stories
1994
King, Martha
QUARTET
PB
248
10.00

Cosima
1991
Cosima
King, Martha
QUARTET
150
5.95

Elias Portulu
1992
Elias Portulu
King, M
QUARTET
PB
192
6.95

Woman and the Priest, The
1987
Madre, La
1920
DEDALUS, SAWTRY
PB
223
5.99

Ashes. A Sardinian story.
1908
Cenere
1904
Colville, H.H
JOHN LANE
307
O/P

DESSI
Giuseppe
Deserter, The
1962
Disertore, Il
1961
Origo, Donata
HARVILL
159
O/P

Forests of Norbio
1975
Paese d'Ombre
1972
Frenaye, F
GOLLANCZ
366

O/P

DONATI
Sergio
Paper Tomb, The
1958
Quigley, I
COLLINS CRIME CLUB
192
O/P

DRIGO
Paola
Maria Zef
1989
Maria Zef
1982
Kirschenbaum, B.
NEBRASKA UP
HB
208
17.95

Maria Zef
1989
Maria Zef
1982
Kirschenbaum, I.S.
NEBRASKA UP
PB
208
8.95

DURANTI
Francesca
Happy Ending
1991
Lieto fine
1987
Cancogni, A
HEINEMANN
HB
164
O/P

Happy Ending
1992
Lieto Fine
1987
Cancogni, A
MINERVA
PB
O/P

House on Moon Lake
1987
Casa sul lago della luna, La
1984
Sartarelli, S
COLLINS HARVIL
HB
O/P

House on Moon Lake
1988
Casa sull lago della luna
1984
Sartarelli, S
FLAMINGO
PB
181
4.99

ECO
Umberto
How to Travel with a Salmon & other Essays
1994
Weaver, W
SECKER & WARBURG
HB
229
9.99

Bomb and the General, The
1989
Weaver, W
SECKER & WARBURG
PB
34
6.95

Foucault's Pendulum
1989
Pendolo di Foucault
1989
SECKER & WARBURG
HB
520
14.95

Foucault's Pendulum
1990
Pendolo di Foucault
1989
PICADOR
PB
656
8.99

Misreadings
1994
Weaver, W
PICADOR
PB
5.99

Misreadings
1994
Weaver, W
CAPE
PB
180
9.99

Name of the Rose, The
1992
Nome della Rosa, Il
1980
MINERVA
PB
6.99

Name of the Rose, The
1992
Nome della Rosa, Il
1980
Weaver, W
MANDARIN
PB
5.99

Name of the Rose, The
1992
Nome della Rosa, Il
1980
Weaver, W
SECKER
512
PB
9.99

Name of the Rose, The
1993
Nome della Rosa, Il
1980
Weaver, W
SECKER & WARBURG
HB
12.95

Name of the Rose,The
1984
Nome della Rosa, Il
1980
Weaver, W
PICADOR
PB
O/P

Three Astronauts, The
1989
Weaver, W
SECKER & WARBURG
PB
34
6.95

EMMANUELLI
Enrico
Black Dove
1964
Green, Peter
BARRIE & ROCKCLIFFE
184
O/P

Man from New Yok, The

1962
Uno da New York
1959
Strachan WJ
MACDONALD
192
O/P

FALLACI
Oriana
Inshallah
1992
Insciallah
1990
Fallaci, O. & Marcus, J
CHATTO
HB
599
15.99

Inshallah
1993
Insciallah
1990
Fallaci, O & J.Marcus
ARROW
PB
775
5.99

Letter to a Child Never Born
1982 (1976)
Lettera a un bambino mai nato
Shepley, J
HAMLYN
PB
O/P

Man, A
1981
Uomo, Un
1980
BODLEY HEAD
HB
O/P

Man, A
1993
Uomo, Un
1980
Weaver, W
ARROW
PB
493
5.99

Man, A
1984 (1981)
HAMLYN
PB
O/P

Penelope at war
1966
Penelope alla guerra
1962
Swinglehurst, Pamela
M JOSEPH
PB
223
O/P

FARINA
Salvatore
From the Foam of the Sea
1879
Marcellina
CHARING CROSS
PUBLISHING CO.
2 vols.
O/P

FELLINI WITH GUERRA
Federico & Tonino
Amarcord. Portrait of a town.
1974
Rootes, Nina
124
O/P

FERRUGGIA
Gemma
Woman's Folly
1895
Zimmern, H.
HEINEMANN
O/P

FLAIANO
Ennio
Time to Kill, A
1992
Tempo di Uccidere
1947
Hood, S
QUARTET
PB
271
7.95

Via Veneto Papers
1995

Satriano, J
MARLBORO P
PB
251
8.99

FOGAZZARO
Antonio
Daniele Cortis
1890
Daniele Cortis
1885
Simeon, S.L.
REMINGTON & CO.:
LONDON,
375
O/P

Little World of the Past
1962
Piccolo Mondo Antico
1895
Strachan, W.J.
OXFORD U.P.: LONDON,
358
O/P

Malombra
1896
Malombra
1881
Dickson, F.T.
UNWIN, T.F.: LONDON,
561
O/P

Man of the World, The
1907
Piccolo Mondo Moderno
1900
Prichard-Agnetti.,M.
HODDER & STOUGHTON.:
LONDON,
356
O/P

Patriot, The
1906
Piccolo Mondo Antico
1895
Agnetti, M.Prichard
HODDER & STOUGHTON.:
LONDON,
433
O/P

Saint, The
1906
Santo, Il
1895
Prichard-Agnetti.,M.
HODDER & STOUGHTON.:
LONDON,
400
O/P

FRATEILI
Arnaldo
Whirlpool, The
1955
Controvento
Moore, David
245
O/P

FRUTTERO, C & LUCENTINI,F
Enigma by the Sea, An
1994
1991
Dowling, Gregory
CHATTO
HB
406
9.99

Sunday Woman, The
1975 (1974)
Donna della Domenica, The
1972
Weaver, W
FONTANA
PB
414
O/P

The D Case: Or the Mystery of Edwin Drood
1995
Donna della Domenica, The
Dowling, G
CHATTO
422
9.99

GADDA
Carlo Emilio
Acquainted with grief
1969
Cognizione del dolore, La
1963
Weaver, W
OWEN
HB
218

That Awful Mess on the Via Merulana
1985
Quer pasticciaccio brutto de via Me
1957
QUARTET
PB
7.95

GHIOTTO
Renato
Slave, The
1969
Scacco alla Regina
1967
Quigley, I
MACDONALD
331
O/P

Slave, The
1970
Scacco alla Regina
1967
Quigley, I
PANTHER
PB
331
O/P

GINZBURG
Natalia
Advertisement, The
1969
Inserzione, L'
Reed, H.
FABER
O/P

All Our Yesterdays
1985
Tutti i nostri ieri
1952
CARCANET
PB
8.95

City and the House, The
1990
Citta e la casa
1985
Davis, D
PALADIN
PB
219
O/P

City and the House, The
1990
Citta e la casa
1985
Davis, Dick
CARCANET
HB
219
O/P

Dear Michael
1975
Caro Michele
1973
Cudahy, Sheila
OWEN
HB
161
10.95

Family & Borghesia, The
1988
Famiglia, La
1977
Stockman, Beryl
CARCANET
HB
111
12.95

Family Sayings
1984
Lessico Famigliare
1963
GRAFTON
PB
O/P

Family Sayings
1967
Lessico Famigliare
1963
CARCANET
HB
12.95

Four Novellas
1990
Cinque romanzi brevi
1965
Bardoni, A & Stockman, B
PALADIN
PB
111
5.99

Little Virtues, The
1985
Piccole Virtu, Le
1962
Davis, D
CARCANET
HB
110
10.95

Manzoni Family, The
Famiglia Manzoni, La
1983
Marie Evans
GRAFTON
PB
O/P

Manzoni Family, The
1987
Famiglia Manzoni, La
1983
Marie Evans
CARCANET
HB
16.95

Never Must You Ask Me

1973
Mai Devi Domandarmi
1970
Quigley, I
M.JOSEPH
HB
168
O/P

Road to the City, The & The Dry Heart
1989
Strada che va in città
1942
Frenaye, F
CARCANET
HB
149
12.95

Valentino & Sagittarius
1987
Cinque Romanzi Breve
1965
Bardoni, A
CARCANET
HB
134
12.95

Voices in the Evening
1990
Le Voci della Sera
1961
Low, D.M.
CARCANET
HB
171
11.95

GIOVANNELLI
Nikolai Leonida
Who Loves His Land; an historical novel of the Garibaldi rising.
1972
STOCKWELL: ILFRACOMBE
448
O/P

GIOVENE
Sansevero I
1987
Autobiografia,L' di Giuliano di Sansevero
Wall, B. et al
QUARTET
PB
631
6.95

Sansevero II
1987

Autobiografia,L' di Giuliano di Sansevero
Wall, B. & W.Riviere
QUARTET
PB
417
6.95

GRAY
Ezio Maria
Bloodless War, The
1917
Guerra senza Sangue
Miall, B
HODDER & STOUGHTON.:
LONDON,
263
O/P

GRAZZI
Vittorio
Hygiene of the Sea
1879
Wright, W.
O/P

GROSSI
Tommaso
Marco Visconti: a novel.
1879
Dugdale, Alice Frances
3 vols.
O/P

GUARESCHI
Giovanni
Comrade Don Camillo
1966
Compagno Don Camillo
Frenaye, F
PENGUIN
PB
158
O/P

Don Camillo and the Devil
1989
ISIS LARGE PRINT BOOKS
HB
6.95

Don Camillo Meets Hell's Angel's
1970
Don Camillo e i giovanni d'oggi
Conrad, L K
GOLLANCZ
HB
173
O/P

Don Camillo Meets Hell's Angel's
1972
Don Camillo e i giovani d'oggi
Conrad, L K
PENGUIN
PB
173
O/P

Don Camillo Omnibus. Little World of D.C., D.C. & the Prodigal Son, Comrade D.C.
1974
Frenaye, F
GOLLANCZ
HB
640
O/P

Don Camilo and the Prodigal Sonl
1952
1952
Frenaye, F
GOLLANCZ
HB
221
O/P

Don Camilo's Dilemma
1954
Frenaye, F
GOLLANCZ
HB
255
O/P

Family Guareschi, The. Chronicles of the Past and Present
1971
Vita in Famiglia
1968
MACDONALD, LONDON
246
O/P

House that Nino built, The
1953
Frenaye, F
GOLLANCZ
HB
223
O/P

Little World of Don Camilo, The
1951
Mondo piccolo di Don Camilo

1948
Troubridge, Una
GOLLANCZ
HB
O/P

GUERCIO, ED.
Francis Michael
Anthology of Contemporary Italian Prose.
1931
Guercio, F.M.
SCHOLARTIS PRESS:
LONDON
197
O/P

GUERRA
Tonino
Equilibrium
1969
Equilibrio, L'
1967
Mosbacher, E
CHATTO
136
O/P

HALL
Robert A (Ed)
Italian Stories
1989
DOVER PB
PB
368
7.95

INZEO, PIERO D' & CORSINI, RENATO
More than victory alone
1970
Guiliani. R.J.
PELHAM BOOKS: LONDON
148
O/P

JAEGGY
Fleur
Sweet Days of Discipline
1991
Beati Anni di Castigo
Parks, T
HEINEMANN
HB
101
12.99

JOVINE
Francesco
Estate in Abruzzi, The
1952

Terre del Sacramento, Le
1950
Colquhoun, A
MACGIBBON & KEE
263
O/P

KEZICH
Lalla
Composition with Dark Centre
1986
Gruppo Concentrico
1985
Gatt, John
OLIVE P: LONDON
HB
165
O/P

Composition with Dark Centre
1986
Gruppo Concentrico
1985
Gatt, John
OLIVE PRESS, LONDON
PB
165
4.95

KING
Martha (Ed.)
New Italian Women; A Collection of Short Fiction
1991
ITALICA P: NY
PB
204
12.95

LA CAPRIA
Raffaele
Mortal Wound, The
1964
COLLINS
191
O/P

LA MALFA
Concetto
Stain on the Sun, A
1993
Macchia nel Sole, Una (Parallel Text)
O Cuilleanáin, C
UNIVERSITY COLLEGE

DUBLIN ITAL DEPT
99
price unknown

LAMPEDUSA
Giuseppe Di
Leopard, The
1988
Gattopardo, Il
1958
A.Colquhoun
COLLINS HARVILL
PB
7.99

Leopard, The
Gattopardo, Il
1958
EVERYMAN
PB
9.99

Leopard, The with A Memory and Two Stories
1991
Gattopardo, Il
1958
COLLINS HARVILL
HB
352
15.50

Two Stories and a Memory
Racconti
1961
PENGUIN
PB
O/P

LANDOLFI
Tommaso
Autumn Story
1989
Racconto d'autunno
1975
Neugroschel, J.
ERIDANOS P.
HB
132
13.95

Autumn Story
1989
Racconto d'autunno
1975
Neugroschel, J.
ERIDANOS P.
PB
132
7.50

Words in Commotion

and Other Stories
1986
Le piu belle pagine di T.L. (mostly from)
1982
Jason, K
PENGUIN
PB
O/P

LEHMANN (ED.)
John
Italian Stories of Today
1959
FABER
265
O/P

LEVI
Carlo
Christ Stopped at Eboli
1982
Christo e fermato a Eboli
1945
Frenaye, F
PENGUIN
PB
253
6.99

Of Fear and Freedom
1950
Paura della Libertà
1946
Gourevitch, Adolphe
CASSELL
HB
101
O/P

Two-fold night, The. A narrative of travel in Germany.
1962
Doppia notte dei tigli, La.
Bernstein, Joseph M
CRESSET PRESS
HB
139
O/P

Watch, The
1952
Orologio, L'
Farrar, J.
CASSELL
PB
296
O/P

LEVI
Primo

Drowned and the Saved, The
1988
Sommersi e i salvati, I
1986
Rosenthal, R
MICHAEL JOSEPH
HB
192
13.99

Drowned and the Saved, The
1989
Sommersi e i salvati, I
1986
Rosenthal, R
ABACUS
PB
170
5.99

If Not Now, When?
1985
Se non ora, quando?
1982
Weaver, W
M. JOSEPH
HB
13.95

If Not Now, When?
1985
Se non ora, quando?
1982
Weaver, W
ABACUS
PB
192
5.99

If This is a Man & The Truce
1979
Se questo e un uomo, La Tregua
1948
Woolf, S
ABACUS
PB
400
6.99

Mirror Maker: Stories and Essay, The
1989
Rosenthal, R
MANDARIN
PB
175
5.99

Mirror Maker: Stories and Essay, The

1989
Rosenthal, R
METHUEN
HB
175
O/P

Moments of Reprieve
1987
Lilit e altri racconti
(mostly)
1981
Feldman, Ruth
ABACUS
PB
176
5.99

Other People's Trades
1989
Altrui mestiere
1985
Rosenthal, R
M JOSEPH
HB
13.99

Other People's Trades
1990
Altrui mestiere
1985
Rosenthal, R
CARDINAL
PB
O/P

Other People's Trades
1991
Altrui mestiere
1985
Rosenthal, R
ABACUS
PB
5.99

Periodic Table, The
1985
Sistema Periodico, Il
1975
Rosenthal, R
ABACUS
PB
240
5.99

Reawakening, The
1965
Tregua, The
1963
Woolf, S
BODLEY HEAD
217
O/P

Sixth Day: and Other

Tales, The
1991
Storie Naturali
1966
Rosenthal, R
ABACUS
PB
6.99

Sixth Day: and Other Tales, The
1991
Storie Naturali
1966
Rosenthal, R
ABACUS
HB
O/P

Wrench, The
1987
Chiave a stella, La
1978
Weaver, W
M JOSEPH
HB
12.99

Wrench, The
1988
Le chiave a stella
1978
Weaver, W
ABACUS
PB
171
5.99

LODOLI
Marco
Innocents, The. Three Tales of Rome
1995
Keys, Roma
QUARTET
PB
320
10.00

LOY
Rosetta
Dust Roads of Monferrato, The
1990
Strade di polvere, Le
Weaver, W
FLAMINGO
PB
251
O/P

Dust Roads of Monferrato, The

1990
Strade di polvere, Le
Weaver, W
HARVILL
HB
O/P

LUGLI
Remo
Shadowed Mind, The
1954
Formiche sotta la fronte, La
Paige, D.D.
OWEN
176
O/P

MAGNANI
Luigi
Beethoven's Nephew
1977
Nipote di Beethoven, Il
Quigley, I
W H ALLEN
120
O/P

MAGRIS
Claudio
Danube, The
1989
Danubio
1986
Creagh, P
COLLINS
HB
416
O/P

Danube, The
1990
Danubio
1986
Creagh, P
COLLINS
PB
8.99

Different Sea, a
1991
Altro Mare, Un
1991
Spurr, M S
COLLINS HARVIL
PB
7.99

Different Sea, A
1993
Altro Mare, Un
1991
Spurr, M S

COLLINS HARVIL
HB
96
12.99

Inferences on a Sabre
1989
Illazioni su una sciabola
1986
Thompson, M
POLYGON
HB
85
5.95

MALAPARTE
Curzio
Kaputt
1964, 1967
Kaputt
1944
Cesare Foligno
PICADOR, PAN
PB
O/P

Skin, The
1952
Pelle, La
1949
Moore, D.
PICADOR
PB
379
O/P

Volga rises in Europe, The
1957
Volga nasce in Europa, Il
1943
Moore, D.
ALVIN REDMAN
281
O/P

MALERBA
Luigi
Serpent, The
1968
Serpente, Il
Weaver, W
H HAMILTON
186
O/P

MANZONI
Alessandro
Betrothed, The
1983
I Promessi Sposi
1840
Penman, B

PENGUIN
PB
720
7.99

MARAINI
Dacia
Age of Discontent, The
1963
Età del malessere, L'
1963
WEIDENFIELD
O/P

Bagheria
1994
Bagheria
Spottiswoode, Elspeth &
Kitto, Dick
OWEN
HB
208
15.50

Holiday, The
1966
Vacanza, La
1962
Hood, S
WEIDENFIELD
176
O/P

Isolina
1993
Isolina, la donna tagliata a pezzi
1985
Williams, Siân
OWEN
HB
152
14.99

Isolina
1995
Isolina, la donna tagliata a pezzi
1985
Williams, Siân
WOMEN'S PRESS
PB
156
6.99

Letters to Marina
1987
Lettere a Marina
1981
Spottiswoode, Elspeth &
Kitto, Dick
CAMDEN P
PB

207
5.95

Letters to Marina
1987
Lettere a Marina
1981
Spottiswoode, Elspeth &
Kitto, Dick
CAMDEN P
HB
207
8.95

Memories of a female thief
1973
Memorie di una ladra
1972
Rootes, Nina
ABELARD SCHUMAN
HB
268
O/P

Memories of a female thief
1975
Memorie di una ladra
1972
Rootes, Nina
NEW ENGLISH LIBRARY
O/P

Silent Duchess, The
1992
Lunga vita di Marianna Ucrià, La
1990
Kitto, D & Spottiswood, E
OWEN
HB
14.99

Silent Duchess, The
1993
Lunga vita di Marianna Ucrià, La
1990
Kitto, D & Spottiswood, E
FLAMINGO
PB
235
5.99

Train, The
1989
Treno per Helsinki, Il
1984
CAMDEN P., LONDON
HB
224

10.95
Train, The
1989
Treno per Helsinki, Il
1984
CAMDEN P., LONDON
PB
5.95

Woman at War
1984
Donna in guerra
Kitto, D & Spottiswood, E
LIGHTHOUSE BOOKS
HB
7.95

Woman at War
1984
Donna in guerra
Kitto, D & Spottiswood, E
LIGHTHOUSE BOOKS
PB
282
4.95

MARCONE
Maria
Woman and her family, A
1987
Analisi in famiglia
Etain Addey
WOMEN'S PRESS
PB
136
O/P

Woman and her family, A
1987
Analisi in famiglia
Etain Addey
WOMEN'S PRESS
HB
136
O/P

MARINETTI
F.T.
Futurist Cookbook
1991
Bull, S
TREFOIL
PB
160
9.95

Futurist Cookbook
1991
Bull, S
TREFOIL
HB
160
14.95

Selected Writings
1972
Various.
Flint, R., Coppotelli, Arthur
SECKER & WARBURG
366
O/P

MAROTTA
Giuseppe
Slaves of Time, The
1964
Alunni del Tempo, Gli
1961
Bridges, Shirley
DOBSON
204
O/P

MARTINI
Plinio
Bottom of the barrel, The
1982
Fondo del Sacco
CALDER SWISS LIBRARY
224
O/P

MARTUCCI, D. & RANIERI, U.
Strange September of 1950
1961
Colquhoun, A
SIDGWICK & JACKSON
126
O/P

MAZZANTINI
Carlo
In Search of a Glorious Death
1992
A cercar la bella morte
1986
Wenkert, S
CARCANET
HB
258
13.95

MAZZETTI
Lorenza
Rage
1965
Con Rabbia

1963
Quigley, I
BODLEY HEAD
221
O/P

Sky Falls, The
1962
Cielo Cade, Il
1961
Waldman, M
BODLEY HEAD
158
O/P

MENEGHELLO
Luigi
Girl called Jules, A
1966
Ragazza di nome Giulio, La
Snell, Graham
HUTCHINSON
O/P

Tantrums
1967
Piccoli maestri, I
1964
Trevelyan, R
M JOSEPH
237
O/P

MESSINA
Maria
House in the Shadows
1991
Casa nel vicolo
1921
Shepley, J
MARLBORO PRESS
133
6.50

MILANI
Milena
Story of Anna Drei, The
1970
Storia di Anna Drei, La
1947
Snell, G
HUTCHINSON
128
O/P

Story of Anna Drei, The
1970
Storia di Anna Drei, La
1947
Snell, G
ARROW
PB

128
O/P

MODICA
Nino
Heart of Stone
1965
Chamberlin, Dennis
ALVIN REDMAN: LONDON,
318
O/P

MONTEROSSO
Carlo
Salt of the Earth, The
1967
Sale della terra, Il
1965
Quigley, I
FABER
191
O/P

MORANTE
Elsa
Arturo's Island
1988 (1959)
Isola di Arturo, L'
1957
Quigley, I
CARCANET
HB
384
14.95

Arturo's Island
1991
Isola di Arturo, L'
1957
Quigley, I
PAN
PB
O/P

History: A Novel
1985 (1980)
Storia
1974
Weaver, W
PENGUIN
PB
730
O/P

History: A Novel
1985 (1980)
Storia
1974
Weaver, W
ALLEN LANE
HB
730
O/P

MORAVIA
Albert
**Bitter Honeymoon &
other stories**
1954
Wall, Bernard
SECKER & WARBURG
HB
221
O/P

Empty Canvas, The
1954
Noia, La
1961
Davidson, A
HB
O/P

1934
1983
1934
1982
SECKER & WARBURG
HB
10.95

**Command and I will
obey you and other
stories**
1969
Cosa è una cosa, Una
1967
Davidson, A
SECKER & WARBURG
HB
190
O/P

**Command and I will
obey you and other
stories**
1970
Cosa è una cosa, Una
1967
Davidson, A
PANTHER
PB
142
O/P

Conformist, The
1952
Conformista, Il
1951
Davidson, Angus
SECKER & WARBURG
349
O/P

Conjugal Love
1964 (1951)
Amore Conjugale
1950

Davidson, Angus
SECKER & WARBURG
HB
O/P

Disobedience
1950
Disubbedienza, La
1948
Davidson, Angus
SECKER & WARBURG
HB
160
O/P

Erotic Tales
Cosa, La ed altri racconti
1983
Parks, T
ABACUS BOOKS, SPHERE
PB
5.99

Erotic Tales
Cosa, La e
1983
Parks, T
SECKER & WARBURG
HB
10.95

Erotic Tales
1987
Cosa, La e
1983
Parks, T
FUTURA
PB
185
O/P

Fancy Dress Party
1954
Mascherata
1947
Angus Davidson
SECKER & WARBURG
HB
O/P

**Fetish, The. A volume of
stories.**
1964
Autonoma, L'
1962
SECKER & WARBURG
HB
285
O/P

Ghost at Noon, A
1983
Disprezzo, Il
1954
PB

251
O/P

Journey to Rome
1993
Viaggio a Roma, Il
1988
Parks, T
ABACUS
PB
5.99

Journey to Rome
1993
Viaggio a Roma, Il
1988
Parks, T
SECKER & WARBURG
HB
O/P

Lady Godiva & other Stories
1973
Altra Vita, Un'
1973
Davidson, A
SECKER & WARBURG
HB
174
O/P

Lie, The
1966
Attenzione, L'
1965
Davidson, A
SECKER & WARBURG
350
O/P

More Roman Tales
O/P

Mother Love
1976
Altra Vita, Un'
1973
Davidson, A
PANTHER
PB
174
O/P

Paradise and other Stories
1969
Paradiso
1967
Davidson, A.
SECKER & WARBURG
HB
190
O/P

Roman Tales
Racconti Romani
1954
OXFORD UP
PB
O/P

Time of Desecration, A
1980
Vita interiore, la
1978
Davidson, A
SECKER & WARBURG
HB
228
10.95

Time of Indifference, The
1953
Indifferenti, Gli
1929
Davidson, A
SECKER & WARBURG
O/P

Time of Indifference, The
1970
Indifferenti, Gli
1929
Davidson, A
PENGUIN
PB
O/P

Two Adolescents
1979
Disubbedienza, La (1950) & Agostino (1947)
1947
Zoete, Beryl de
PANTHER
PB
O/P

Two Women
1983
SECKER & W
HB
O/P

Voice of the Sea
1978
Boh
1976
A.Davidson
SECKER & W
HB
224
10.95

Voice of the Sea
1981
Boh
1976
Davidson, A.

PANTHER
PB
O/P

Voyeur, The
1986
Uomo che guarda, L'
1985
Parks, T
SECKER & WARBURG
HB
208
O/P

Voyeur, The
1991
Uomo che guarda, L'
1985
Parks, T
ABACUS
PB
185
O/P

Voyeur, The
Uomo che guarda, L'
1985
Parks, T
FUTURA
PB
208
3.99

Wayward Wife, The
1963
Davidson, A
PENGUIN
PB
216
O/P

Wheel of Fortune
1938
Ambizioni Sbagliate, Le
1935
Livingston, Arthur
CASSELL & CO
549
O/P

Woman of Rome, The
1949
Romana, La
1947
Holland, Lydia
SECKER & WARBURG
389
O/P

MORAZZONI
Marta
Girl in a Turban
1990
Ragazza col turbante, La
1986

Creagh, P
HARVILL
PB
157
5.95

Girl in a Turban
1990
Ragazza col turbante, La
1986
Creagh, P
HARVILL
HB
157
O/P

His Mother's House
1994
Casa Materna
1992
Rose, Emma
HARVILL
PB
112
7.99

His Mother's House
1994
Casa Materna
1992
Rose, Emma
HARVILL
HB
112
13.99

MORSELLI
Guido
Divertimento 1889
1986
Divertimento 1889
1975
Shankland, Hugh
CHATTO
HB
145
O/P

**Past Conditional: A
Retrospective**
1990
Contro-passato prossimo
1975
Shankland, H
CHATTO
HB
249
O/P

OLIVERO
Luigi
Adam & Eve in America
1951

Adamo ed Eva in America
1946
Warren, Ivy
MACDONALD
173
O/P

**OLIVIERI
SANGIACOMO**
Arturo
**Colonel, The, a military
romance**
1904
Spender, E.
PHOENIX LIBRARY
340
O/P

ONGARO
Alberto
Excelsior
1967
Complice, Il
1965
Cremonesi, Giles &
O'Donnell, S
BODLEY H
205
O/P

ORSERI
Remo
**Jerusalem, prisoner of
hope**
1978
*Tikva, porta della
speranza*
1974
WAYLAND: HOVE
268
O/P

ORTESE
Anna-Maria
Bay is not Naples, The
1955
Mare non bagna Napoli, Il
1953
Frenaye, Francis
COLLINS
189
O/P

Iguana, The
1987
Iguana, L'
1965
Martin, Henry
MINERVA
PB
197
O/P

OTTIERI
Ottiero
Men at the gate, The
1962
Donnarumma all'assalto
1959
Rawson, I.M.
GOLLANCZ
244
O/P

PALANDRI
Enrico
Ages Apart
Pietre e Sale
COLLINS HARVIL
HB
191
O/P

Way Back, The
1993
Via del Ritorno, La
1990
Hood, S
SERPENT'S TAIL
PB
169
8.99

PALAZZESCHI
Aldo
Materassi Sisters
1953
Sorelle Materassi
1934
Davidson, A
SECKER & WARBURG
300
O/P

PALLADINO
Giuliano
Peace at Alamein
1962
Pace a El Alamein
1960
Trevelyan, Raleigh
HODDER
318
O/P

PALUMBO
Nino
Bribe, The
1960
Impiegato d'Imposte
1956
Quigley, I
HARVILL
318

database of Italian fiction translated in UK

Tomorrow will be better
1965
Pane verde
1961
Quigley, I
HARVILL
253
O/P

PAPINI
Giovanni
Failure, The
(1924 1st ed)1973
Uomo finito, un
1912
GREENWOOD P
HB
32.50

PARISE
Goffredo
Abecedary, The
1991
Silibario, Il
1982
Marcus, J
MARLBORO PRESS
PB
147
7.99

Boss, The
1967
Padrone, Il
1965
Weaver, W
CAPE
O/P

Solitudes: Short Stories
1984
Sillabario 2
1982
Quigley, I
DENT
PB
173
O/P

PASOLINI
Pier Paolo
Dream of Something, A
1988
Sogno di una Cosa, Il
1962
Hood, S
QUARTET
PB
129
5.95

Letters, 1940-45
1992
Lettere
QUARTET
HB
526
25

Lutheran Letters
1983
Lettere Luterane
1976
Hood, S
CARCANET
HB
129
12.95

Ragazzi, The
1986
Ragazzi di Vita, I
1955
Capouya, Emile
CARCANET
256
12.95

Roman Nights and Other Stories
1991
Alì dagli occhi azzurri (5 stories from)
1965
Shepley, J
MARLBORO PRESS
PB
134
O/P

Roman Nights and Other Stories
1994
Alì dagli occhi azzurri (5 stories from)
1965
Shepley, J
QUARTET
PB
134
9.00

Roman Poems
1986
Ferlinghetti, L & Valente, F
CITY LIGHTS
PB
128
4.95

Theorem
1992
Teorema
1968
Hood, S
QUARTET
PB
182
6.95

Violent Life, A
1985
Vita Violenta, Una
1959
Weaver, W
CARCANET
PB
9.95

PATTI
Ercole
Cousin Agata
Cugina, La
1965
Edwards, Lovett
159
O/P

Love Affair in Rome, A
1958
Amore a Roma, Un
1956
Fitzgibbon, C
CHATTO
159
O/P

Roman Chronicle
1962
O/P

That Wonderful November
1967
Bellisimo Novembre, Un
1967
Quigley, I
CHATTO
112
O/P

PAVESE
Cesare
Among Women Only
1990
Tra Donne Sole
1953
Paige, D.D
SCEPTRE
PB
159
O/P

Beach, The
1963

Spiaggia, La
1941
OWEN
O/P

Business of Living, This
1980 (1961)
Mestiere di vivere, il
1952
Murch, A E
QUARTET
PB
O/P

Devil in the Hills
1954
*Diavolo sulle colline, La
bella estate*
1949
Paige, D.D
OWEN
HB
14.95

Devil in the Hills
1990
*Diavolo sulle colline, La
bella estate*
1949
Paige, D.D
SCEPTRE
PB
4.99

Festival Night
1964
Notte di Festa
1953
Murch, A E
OWEN
HB
211
14.95

Harvesters, The
1961
Paesi Tuoi
1941
O/P

Leather Jacket
*Selection from; Summer
Storm & Festival Night*
1953
QUARTET
PB
O/P

**Moon and the Bonfire,
The**
1988
Luna e il falò, La
1950
Sinclair, L

SCEPTRE
PB
192
5.99

Political Prisoner, The
1969
Carcere, Il
Strachan, W.J.
OWEN
HB
237
14.95

**Selected Letters 1924-
1950**
1969
Murch, A E
OWEN
HB
270
15.95

**Summer Storm & Other
Stories**
1966
*Racconti di Cesare Pavese
(Selection?)*
1960
Murch, A E
OWEN
HB
216
14.95

**Told in Confidence &
other Stories**
1971
*Racconti: (1960)+ Cesare
Pavese: Racconti (1968)*
1960
Murc h, A.E.
OWEN
HB
155
O/P

PAZZI
Roberto
Adrift in Time
1991
Malattia del Tempo
Vivien Sinott
DEUTSCH
HB
176
12.99

Princess and Dragon
1990
Principessa, La e il drago
DEUTSCH
HB
162

12.99
**Searching for the
Emperor**
Cercando l'imperatore
1985
Fitzgerald, M.
PICADOR
PB
O/P

**Searching for the
Emperor**
1989
Cercando L'Imperatore
1985
Fitzgerald, M.
DEUTSCH
HB
196
10.95

PERRI
Francesco
Unknown Disciple, The
1950
Discepolo Ignoto, The
Russel, H.T.
BLES.
416

PETRIGNANI
Sandra
Toy Catalogue,The
1990
Catalogo dei Giocattoli, Il
1988
Lombardo, Ray
BOULEVARD: DIST. BY
CENTRAL BOOKS
PB
128
5.95

PICCHIO
Carlo
Freedom Fighter
1980
Scarola
1965
OUP
O/P

PIOVENE
Guido
Confessions of a Novice
1950
Lettere di un novizia
1941
KIMBER
194
O/P

PIRANDELLO
Luigi
Better think twice about it & 12 other stories
1933
Mayne, A & H
JOHN LANE
309
O/P

Eleven Short Stories
1994
(Parallel Text Edition)
Appelbaum, S
CONSTABLE
187
8.95

Late Mattia Pascal, The
1988
Il fu Mattia Pascal
1904
Simborowski, N
DEDALUS, SAWTRY
PB
6.99

Late Mattia Pascal, The
1988
Il fu Mattia Pascal
1904
Simborowski, N
DEDALUS, SAWTRY
HB
10.95

Late Mattia Pascal, The
1988
Il fu Mattia Pascal
1904
Weaver, W
ERIDANOS
HB
15.50

Late Mattia Pascal, The
1988
Il fu Mattia Pascal
1904
Weaver, W
ERIDANOS
PB
8.95

Late Mattia Pascal, The
1993
Il fu Mattia Pascal
1904
Weaver, W
DEUTSCH
PB

262
9.99
Naked Truth, The
1934
Novelle per un Anno
(Selection from)
Mayne, A & H
JOHN LANE
308
O/P

Notebooks of Serafino Gubbio
1990
Quaderni di Serafino Gubbio
Scott-Moncrief
DEDALUS, SAWTRY
PB
334
7.99

One, None and a Hundred Thousand.
Uno, Nessuno e Centomila
1926
Weaver, W
ERIDANOS
HB
15.95

One, None and a Hundred Thousand.
1989 (1933)
Uno, Nessuno e Centomila
1926
Weaver, W
ERIDANOS
PB
8.95

Short Stories
1987
May, F
QUARTET
PB
266
5.95

Short Stories.
1965
Frederick May
OXFORD
260
O/P

Tales of Madness, A Selection from 'Short Stories for a Year'
1984
DANTE U. OF AMERICA
Bussino, G
HB
147

13.50
Tales of Suicide, A Selection from 'Short Stories for a Year'
1988
Bussino, G
DANTE U. OF AMERICA
PB
147
10.99

PIRRO
Ugo
Five Branded Women
1960
Jovanka e le altre
1959
Hochman, Stanley
POCKET BKS (THORPE & P: LEICESTER)
182
O/P

PITIGRILLI
Cocaine
1982
Cocaina
Mosbacher, E
HAMLYN PABERBACKS
PB
205
O/P

Mr. Pott
1933
Esperimento di Pott, L'
Wells, Warre B
JOHN LANE
312
O/P

POMILIO
Mario
New Line, The
1961
Nuovo Corso
1959
Colquhoun, A
142
O/P

PONTIGGIA
Giuseppe
Invisible Player
1988
Giocatore invisibile, il
1978
Cancogni, A
ERIDANOS
PB
224

8.50

Invisible Player
1988
Giocatore invisibile, il
1978
Cancogni, A
ERIDANOS
HB
224
15.50

PORTA
Antonio
King of the Storeroom, The
1992
1978
Smith, Lawrence R
WESLEYAN/NEW ENGLAND
UP
149
15.95

Passenger
1986
Verdicchio, P
GUERNICA EDITIONS,
CANADA
PB
6.50

POZZA
N
Sacred and the Profane
1979
GORDON & CREMOVESI:
LONDON
280
O/P

PRATOLINI
Vasco
Bruno Santini
1965
Costanza della Ragione, La
1965
Rosenthal, R
CHATTO
313
O/P

Family Chronicle
1991
Cronaca Familiare
1947
QUARTET
PB
121
5.95

Hero of Today, A
1951

Eroe di nostro tempo, un
1949
Mosbacher, E
HAMILTON, H
250
O/P

Metello
1968
Metello
1960
Rosenthal, R
283
O/P

Tale of Santa Croce
1952
Quartiere, Il
1944
Duncan, P & P
OWEN
254
O/P

PRESSBURGER
Giorgio
Teeth
1996
Spence, P
PENGUIN
HB
192
13.99

PRESSBURGER
Giorgio & Nicola
Green Elephant, The
1994
1988
Spence, Piers
QUARTET
PB
113
9.00

Homage to the Eighth District
1990
Storie del Ottavo Distretto
1986
Moore, Gerald
READERS INTERNATIONAL
HB
134
10.95

Homage to the Eighth District
1990
Storie del Ottavo Distretto
1986
Moore, Gerald
READERS INTERNATIONAL

PB
134
5.95

Law of White Spaces, The
1992
Legge degli spazi bianchi
1989
Spence, Piers
GRANTA
HB
O/P

Law of White Spaces, The
1993
Legge degli spazi bianchi
1989
Spence, Piers
GRANTA
PB
5.99

PRISCO
Michele
Heirs of the Wind
1953
Eredi del Vento, Gli
1951
Macdonald, V.M.
VERSCHOYLE
HB
462
O/P

Spiral of Mist
1969
Spirale di Nebbia, Una
1966
Quigley, I
CHATTO
HB
O/P

QUINAVALLE
Uberto Paolo
On the make
1962
Capitale mancata
1959
Quigley, I
HARVILL
190
O/P

RAMONDINO
Fabrizia
Althenopis
1988
Althenopis
Michael Sullivan
CARCANET
HB
220
14.95

REA
Domenico
Blush of Shame, A
1963
Vampata di Rossore
1959
Duffy, M
BARRIE & ROCKCLIFF
222
O/P

RIPELLINO
Angelo Mario
Magic Prague
1994
Marinelli, D N
MACMILLAN
HB
O/P

Magic Prague
1994
Marinelli, D N
PICADOR
PB
333
9.99

ROBERTO
Federico De
Viceroys, The
1989
Viceri, I
A.Colquhoun
COLLINS HARVILL
PB
627
7.95

ROCCA
Guido
Indiscretion
1958
Ragazza Impudente, La
Moore, David
241
O/P

ROSSO
Renzo
Bait and other stories,

The
1962
Adescamento, L'
1959
Colquhoun, A
SECKER & WARBURG
174
O/P

Hard Thorn, The
1966
Dura Spina, La
1963
Weaver, W
ROSS: LONDON
301
O/P

RUGARLI
Giannpaolo
Crux, The
1990
Troga, La
N.S.Thompson
COLLINS HARVILL
HB
O/P

SABA
Umberto
Ernesto
1987
Thompson, Mark
CARCANET
HB
144
12.95

Ernesto
1989
Thompson, Mark
PALADIN ne. GRAFTON
PB
O/P

Stories and Recollections
1993
Gibson, E
SHEEP MEADOW PRESS,
USA
PB
256
9.95

SALVALAGGIO
Nantas
Moustache, The
1962
Baffo, Il
1961
Sprigge, Sylvia
MACDONALD
174

O/P

SAMONA
Carmelo
Brothers
1992
Fratelli
Linda Lappin
CARCANET
HB
180
13.95

SATTA
Salvatore
Day of Judgement
Giorno del Giudizio, Il
Creagh, P
COLLINS HARVILL
HB
298
O/P

Day of Judgement
Giorno del Giudizio, Il
Creagh, P
COLLINS HARVILL
PB
298
7.99

SAVIANE
Giorgio
Finger in the candle flame, The
1964
Papa, Il
1963
Edwards, Lovett
ALLEN & UNWIN
248
O/P

SAVINIO
Alberto
Capri
1991
Capri
1988
Shepley, J
MARLBORO P
PB
4.95

Childhood of Nivasio Dolcemare
1941
Infanzia di Nivasio Dolcemare
1982
ERIDANOS
PB

O/P

Childhood of Nivasio Dolcemare
1941
Infanzia di Nivasio Dolcemare
1995
QUARTET
PB
168
9.00

Childhood of Nivasio Dolcemare
1941
Infanzia di Nivasio Dolcemare
1982
ERIDANOS
HB
13.95

Lives of the Gods
1991
Vita dei Fantasmi
Brook, J & Erdlinger, S
ATLAS
PB
144
6.99

Operatic Lives
1991
Shepley, J
MARLBORO P
PB
8.99

Speaking to Clio
1993
Dico a te, Clio
1940
Shepley, J
MARLBORO P
PB
140
6.95

SCANZIANI
Piero
Adventure of Man
1991
EUREKA
HB
272
14.99

Entronauts; the Journey within
1991
EUREKA

HB
232
14.99

Man for Europe, A
1991
EUREKA
HB
300
9.99

White Book, the
1991
Libro Bianco
EUREKA
HB
307
9.99

SCERBANENCO
Giorgio
Duca and the Milan murders
1970
Traditori di tutti
1966
Ellenbogen, Ellen
CASSELL
214
O/P

Duca and the Milan murders
1972
Traditori di tutti
1966
Ellenbogen, Ellen
CORGI
PB
214
O/P

SCIASCIA
Leonardo
1912 + 1
1989
Sacha Rabinovitch
CARCANET
HB
133
12.95

Candido: Or, a Dream dreamed in Italy
1979
Candido
1977
CARCANET
PB
O/P

Candido: Or, a Dream dreamed in Italy
1994

Candido
1977
HARVILL
PB
144
7.99

Council of Egypt
1966
Consiglio d'Egitto
1963
Foulke, Adrienne
CARCANET
HB
212
12.95

Council of Egypt
1993
Consiglio d'Egitto
1963
Foulke, Adrienne
HARVILL
PB
212
8.99

Day of the Owl
Giorno della Civetta, Il
1961
Colquhoun, A & Oliver, A
CARCANET
HB
8.95

Day of the owl
1987
Giorno della civetta, Il
1961
Colquhoun, A & Oliver, A
PALADIN
PB
4.99

Death of An Inquisitor and Other Stories, The
1990
Morte dell'Inquisitatore
CARCANET
HB
12.95

Death of An Inquisitor and Other Stories, The
1994
Morte dell'Inquisitatore
Thomson, Ian
HARVILL
PB
192
8.99

Death of An Inquisitor and Other Stories, The
Morte dell'Inquisitatore
Thomson, Ian
GRAFTON
PB
192
5.99

Knight and Death and other Stories, The
1992
Storia Semplice, Porte Aperte, Il Cavaliere et al
Farrell, Joe & Evans, Marie
HARVILL
PB
7.99

Knight and Death and other Stories, The
1991
Storia Semplice, Porte Aperte, Il Cavaliere et al
Farrell, Joe & Evans, Marie
CARCANET
HB
215
12.95

Moro Affair, The and the Mystery of Majorana
1987
Affaire Moro, L' &
Rabinivitch, S
CARCANET
HB
200
12.95

One Way or Another
1987
Todo Modo
Sacha Rabinovitch
CARCANET
HB
12.95

One Way or Another
1989
Todo Modo
Rabinovitch, Sacha
GRAFTON
PB
103
3.99

Salt in the Wound
1969
Parrochie di Regalpetra
1956

O/P
Sicilian Uncles
1986
Zii di Sicilia, Gli
Thompsom, N S
CARCANET
HB
210
12.95

Sicilian Uncles
1988
Zii di Sicilia, Gli
GRAFTON
PB
O/P

To Each His Own
1992
A Ciascuno il Suo
1968
Foulke, A
CARCANET
HB
O/P

To Each His Own
1989
A Ciascuno il suo
1968
Adrienne Foulke
CARCANET
PB
146
O/P

To Each His Own
1992
A Ciascuno il suo
1968
Adrienne Foulke
BLACK & WHITE
PB
146
5.95

Wine-dark Sea
1988
Mare Colore del Vino, Il
1973
Bardoni, Avril
CARCANET
HB
O/P

Wine-dark Sea
1988
Mare Colore del Vino, Il
1973
Bardoni, Avril
GRAFTON
PB
O/P

SECCO
Nicolo
Inganni
UNIV. OF EXETER
PB
O/P

SERAO
Matilde
After the Pardon
1909
Dopo il Perdono
1904
EVERLEIGH NASH:
LONDON
334
O/P

Conquest of Rome, The
1991 (1902)
Conquista di Roma
PICKERING & CHATTO
246
24.95

Desire of Life, The
1911
Collinge, Wm.
STANLEY PAUL: LONDON
320
O/P

Fantasy
1890
Fantasia
1883
H.H.
HEINEMANN'S INTERNATIONAL LIBRARY
O/P

Farewell Love!
1890
Harland, Mrs. M.
HEINEMANN'S INTERNATIONAL LIBRARY
280
O/P

In the Country of Jesus.
1905
Davey, R.
HEINEMANN: LONDON
294
O/P

Land of Cockayne, The
1901, 1971
Paese di Cuccagna, Il
1891
HEINEMANN
HB
369
O/P

SERVADIO
Gaia
Melinda
1968
*Tanto gentile e tanto
onesta*
1967
Conrad, L K
WEIDENFELD
HB
319
O/P
Melinda
1969
*Tanto gentile e tanto
onesta*
1967
Conrad, L K
PANTHER
319
O/P
Story of R, The
1994
Mostyn-Owen, Allegra
PAN
PB
213
3.99

SGORLON
Carlo
Wooden Throne, The
1991
Trono di Legno, Il
ITALICA PRESS, US
PB
320
11.99

SILONE
Ignazio
Bread and Wine
Vino e Pane
Mosbacher, E
DENT
PB
272
O/P

Fontamara
1985
Fontamara
1933
Mosbacher, Eric
DENT: LONDON
HB
180
O/P
Fontamara
1994

Fontamara
1933
Mosbacher, Eric
REDWORDS
PB
180
6.50
Fontamara
1994
Fontamara
1933
Mosbacher, Eric
EVERYMAN
PB
180
4.99
Fox and the Camellias
1961
Volpe e le camelle, Le
1960
Mosbacher, Eric
160
O/P
**Handful of blackberries,
A**
1954
Manciata di more, una
1952
Silone, Darina
CAPE
288
O/P
School for Dictators, The
1939
Scuola dei dittatori
1938
Mosbacher, E & David,
Gwenda
CAPE
PB
303
O/P
**Seed beneath the Snow,
The**
1942, 1957
Seme sotto la neve, Il
1941
Frenaye, F
CAPE
HB
384
O/P

SIMONETTA
Umberto
Shrimp, The
1962
Barren, Diana
H HAMILITON

158
O/P
SOLDATI
Mario
American Bride
Sposa americana, La
1977
HODDER
HB.
O/P
**Commander comes to
dinner, The**
1952
A Cena col commendatore
1950
LEHMANN
223
O/P
Orange Envelope, The
1969
Busta Arancione, La
1960
Wall, B
DEUTSCH
223
O/P
Real Silvestri, The
1960
Vero Silvestri, Il
1957
Colquhoun, A
DEUTSCH
188
O/P

SOLINAS
Franco
Squarcio, the Fisherman
1958
Frenaye, F
HUTCHINSON
139
O/P

SPINA
Michele
West of the Moon
1994
Occidente della Luna, Ad
Colcord, Ann
OWEN
PB
99
8.95

STEFANI

Livia De

Rosa
1963
Passione di Rosa
1958
Barford, C & Hodge, S
EYRE & SPOTTISWOODE
230
O/P

STRATI
Saverio
Empty Hands
1963
Mani Vuote
Moule, Peter
ABELARD-SCHUMAN
265
O/P

Lights of Reggio, The
1965
Avventura in città
1962
Davidson, A
MURRAY
206
O/P

Terrarossa
1962
Teda, La
1957
Ellman, Elizabeth
ABELARD-SCHUMAN
223
O/P

SVEVO
Italo
As a Man Grows Older
1993
Senilità
1932
Zoete, Beryl de
PENGUIN
PB
5.99

Confessions of Zeno
Coscienza di Zeno
1923
SECKER & WARBURG
HB
O/P

Confessions of Zeno
Coscienza di Zeno
1923
SECKER & WARBURG
PB
O/P

Hoax, The

1929
Burla Riuscita, Una
1928
Zoete, B. de
WOOLF, LEONARD &
VIRGINIA
24
O/P

Life, A
1991
Vita, Una
1892
PENGUIN
PB
6.99

Short Sentimental Journey & other stories. (The Hoax/Story of the Old Man & the Pretty Girl/Generous Wine/The Mother/ Argo & his Master/Short Sentimental Journey/Death)
1967
SECKER
319
O/P

TABUCCHI
Antonio
Indian Nocturne
1991
Notturno Indiano
118
VINTAGE
PB
O/P

Little Misunderstandings of No Importance
Piccoli Equivoci senza importanza
1985
CHATTO
HB
139
O/P

Little Misunderstandings of no Importance
1991
Piccoli Equivoci senza importanza
1985
VINTAGE
PB
4.99

Requiem
1994
Requiem

1991
Costa, M J
HARVILL
HB
112
14.99

Requiem
1994
Requiem
1991
Costa, M J
HARVILL
PB
112
7.99

Vanishing Point
1991
Filo d'Orrizonte, Donna di Porto Pim, Volatili del Beato Angelico
1986
Parks, T
CHATTO
HB
257
O/P

Vanishing Point
1993
Filo d'Orrizonte, Donna di Porto Pim, Volatili del Beato Angelico
1986
Parks, T
VINTAGE
PB
257
4.99

TALBOT, & MARIANACCI
Ed.s
George & Dante
Short Stories from Abruzzo
1993
Various
IRISH ACADEMIC
PB
172
7.50

TESTORI
Giovanni
House in Milan, The
1963
Alexander, Sidney
COLLINS
O/P

TOBINO

Mario
Underground, The
1966
Clandestino, Il
1962
Rosenthal, R
HEINEMANN
O/P

TONDELLI
Pier Vittorio
Separate Rooms
1992
Camere separate, Le
1989
Pleasance, Simon
SERPENT'S TAIL
PB
186
8.99

TOZZI
Federigo
Eyes Shut
1990
Con gli occhi chiusi
1919
Kenneth Cox
CARCANET
HB
171
12.95

Three Crosses
1921
Tre Croce
1920
Capellero, R
SECKER & WARBURG
HB
173
O/P

TREVELYAN Ed.
Raleigh
**Italian Short Stories/
Racconti Italiani I**
1986
var.
PENGUIN
PB
198
5.99

Italian Writing Today
1967
Various
PENGUIN
PB
285
O/P

VARE

Daniele
**Maker of heavenly
trousers, The**
1986
BLACK SWAN
217
O/P
**Temple of Costly
Experience, The**
1988
BLACK SWAN
PB
238
O/P

VASSALLI
Sebastiano
Chimera, The
1994
Chimera, La
1990
Creagh, P
HARVILL
HB
314
15.99

Night of the Comet
1989
Notte della cometa, La
Gatt, John
CARCANET
HB
220
12.95

VENTURI
Marcello
White Flag, The
1966
*Bandiera bianca a
Cefalonia*
1963
Clover, Wm.
BLOND
191
O/P

VERALDI
Attilio
Payoff, The
1978
Mazetta, La
1976
Quigley, I
H.HAMILTON
234
O/P

VERGA
Giovanni

Cavalleria Rusticana
1987
Lawrence, D H
DEDALUS, SAWTRY
PB
5.99
**House by the Medlar
Tree**
Malavoglia, I
GREENWOOD
HB
O/P
**House by the Medlar
Tree**
Malavoglia, I
1881
Landry, J
DEDALUS, SAWTRY
PB
7.99
**House by the Medlar
Tree**
1984
Malavoglia, I
1881
Rosenthal, R
CALIFORNIA U P
HB
275
30.00
**House by the Medlar
Tree**
1984
Malavoglia, I
1881
Rosenthal, R
CALIFORNIA U P
PB
275
10.50
Little Novels of Sicily
Novelle rusticane
Lawrence, D.H.
GREENWOOD PRESS,
LONDON
HB
O/P
Maestro Don Gesualdo
Maestro Don Gesualdo
1888
Lawrence, D.H.
GREENWOOD
HB
34.50
Maestro Don Gesualdo
Maestro Don Gesualdo
1888
Lawrence, D H

Maestro Don Gesualdo
1984
Maestro Don Gesualdo
1888
Cecchetti, G
CALIFORNIA UP
PB
348
8.95

She-Wolf and other stories
1984
Cecchetti, G
CALIFORNIA UP
PB
316
6.90

Short Sicilian Novels
Novelle Rusticane
Lawrence, D H
DEDALUS, SAWTRY
PB
176
6.99

Sparrow: Story of a Songbird
1994
Storia di una Capinera
1871
Donougher, C
DEDALUS, SAWTRY
PB
177
6.99

VIGANÒ
Valeria
Run!
1996
*Tennis nel Bosco, Il +
addit. storie*
1989
Lombardo, Ray
BOULEVARD: DIST.
CENTRAL BOOKS
PB
6.95

VITTORINI Ed.
Dimitri
**Italian Short Stories/
Racconti Italiani II**
1972
var.
PENGUIN
PB
198
5.99

VITTORINI

Elio
Conversation in Sicily
1988
*Conversazione in Sicilia.
Nome e lacrime.*
1941
Wilfrid David
QUARTET
PB
134
5.95

**Dark and the Light,The
'Erica' & Garibaldina, La**
*Erica e suoi fratelli, La
Garabaldina*
1956
GREENWOOD PRESS
HB
O/P

Red Carnation
1952
Garofano Rosso
1948
Bower, A.
GREENWOOD P
HB
O/P

**Woman on the roads,
Erica, La Garabaldina.**
1961
Keene, F & Wall, B
CAPE
240
O/P

Women of Messina
1975
Donne di Messina, Le
1964
Frenaye, F
LONDON MAGAZINE
EDITIONS; LONDON
PB
307
O/P

VOLPINI
Flora
Woman of Florence, The
1966 (1955)
Moore, David
MAYFLOWER
PB
O/P

Yes madam
1964
Commandi Signore
1961
Oliver, Arthur
REDMAN

207
O/P

VOLPONI
Paolo
Memorandum, The
1973
Memoriale, Il
1962
SEVEREID, B
MARION BOYARS
PB
5.95

Memorandum, The
1968
Memoriale, Il
Severeid, B
MARION BOYARS
HB
13.95

Worldwide Machine, The
1969
Macchina Mondiale, La
1965
Severeid, Belen
MARION BOYARS
213
13.95

VOLTA
Ornella
Vampire, The
1970
Vampire, Le
Rudorff, Raymond
TANDEM: LONDON
158
O/P

WALDMAN Ed.
G.
**Penguin Book of Italian
Short Stories**
1969
PENGUIN
PB
335
O/P

WERTMULLER
Lina
Head of Alvise, The
1983
Testa di Alvise
HEINEMANN
255
O/P

ZANGRANDI
Ruggiero
Train to Brenner, A
1963
Tradotta del Brennero, La
1960
Wolcott-Belinke, Roger
GALLEY PRESS
288
O/P

Babel Guides on Disk:

The Italian Fiction in English Translation Database is available to bona fide Researchers and Libraries on 3½ inch diskettes in DOS.txt or DBF format, £50 post free. Regular updates to include titles and reviews entered since publication date can be provided to subscribers.

Babel Guide to fiction from FRANCE

A unique guide to novels and short stories by French writers of the 20th Century translated into English.
All the best books are reviewed with additional feature pieces on writers.

Use the listings and reviews to choose books to read available in your bookshop or library and put a new world of writing at your fingertips.

- ➤ Original reviews & features
- ➤ Covers books 1945–1996
- ➤ 45 illustrations
- ➤ 500+ books and editions listed

192 pages   £7.95
ISBN 1899460 11 X Spring 1996

Babel Guide
to fiction from
Portugal
Brazil
& Africa
in translation

A unique guide to novels and short stories from Portugal, Brazil, Angola and Mozambique translated into English. All the best books are reviewed with additional feature pieces on writers.

Use it in bookshop or library to put a new world of writing at your fingertips.

➢ Original reviews & features
➢ Covers books 1945–1996
➢ 17 illustrations
➢ 184 books and editions listed

144 pages   £7.95
ISBN 1899460 06 3 Autumn 1995

the toy catalogue

by Sandra Petrignani

The *Toy Catalogue* is a compendium of childhood passions — the smell of plasticine, the lickability of play-nails and the comforting hug of your rag doll. A genial Gulliverian hand picks you up and lets you fall into the deepest seas of childhood.
Guaranteed to take you back to the delicious intensities of childhood, on a wonderful and healing journey.

Winner of the Bergamo Prize in 1989.

'An enchanting exercise in playfulness'
Ian McEwan

Boulevard Italians

128p £5.95

All the Babel Guides and Boulevard's world fiction titles are available in good bookshops or direct from the publisher; post and packing free in the European Union, elsewhere add 10%.

 UK Cheques or Eurocheques in Sterling or US dollar cheques on major New York or California banks are accepted, made out to Boulevard.

If you are interested in contemporary world fiction please ask to join our mailing list.

Orders & Enquiries to;
Boulevard, 8 Aldbourne Road, London W12 OLN UK.
Tel/Fax: 0181-743-5278